Chris Humphries

more to life

D0488713

DENNIS PETHERS

more
to life

Reaching people with the true message of Jesus

Copyright © Dennis Pethers 2005

Published 2005 by CWR, Waverley Abbey House, Waverley Lane, Farnham, Surrey GU9 8EP.

The right of Dennis Pethers to be identified as the author of this work has been asserted by him in accordance with the Copyright, Designs and Patents Act 1988.

All rights reserved. No part of this publication may be reproduced, stored in a retrieval system, or transmitted, in any form or by any means, electronic, mechanical, photocopying, recording or otherwise, without the prior permission in writing of CWR.

See back of book for list of National Distributors.

Unless otherwise indicated, all Scripture references are from the *Holy Bible: New International Version* (NIV), copyright © 1973, 1978, 1984 by the International Bible Society.

Front cover image: PhotoDisc

Concept development, editing, design and production by CWR

Printed in Finland by WS Bookwell

ISBN 1-85345-347-1

Contents

Introduction   7

Part 1   **The Moment**

1   Who's the bloke on the wall?   11
2   Who's the bloke on the street?   15

Part 2   **The Message**

3   Jesus – the message is announced   31
4   The apostles – the message is revealed   45
5   After the apostles – the message is concealed   63
6   The Reformation – the message is rediscovered   81
7   From message to method   91

Part 3   **The Method**

8   Change for good   107
9   Witnessing communities   127
10 Witnessing Christians   147

Appendix   165
Notes   167

Introduction

Sitting on a train outside Liverpool Street Station, London, in the mid 1970s, I became a Christian. I had never been to church in my life but suddenly, as a result of reading *Mere Christianity*, a book that my boss had given to me, my life was changed. I was so thrilled by the good news I had discovered that I immediately wanted to tell people about Jesus ... so I did!

I soon discovered that it was usual for Christians to attend church, so I went to the one nearest my home. I came into contact with a group of people that were kind and loving but somehow different from anyone I had ever met before. They all seemed to gain so much comfort and fulfilment from all of the things that went on in the church but for me it was all so strange. Increasingly I found it difficult to see any relationship between what I read in the Bible and what happened in the church. I also just couldn't see the relevance of much that happened, I so wanted to take my friends along but I knew it wouldn't make sense to them ... so I didn't!

Years on I am an evangelist that has visited far more churches than I can remember. I now have a greater passion to tell people about Jesus and an even bigger conviction that the Church must do things differently if it is going to make sense to people today.

In the days in which we live, the message of Jesus is still as relevant as ever. As we discover the freedom to express this message in creative and relevant ways, and as Christian communities remember that they exist in order to make this message known, things will change.

I have written this book to encourage, not to be critical or to apportion blame. My prayer, as you read it, is that God will thrill you again with the opportunity that is before us.

PART 1

The
Moment

1

Who's the bloke on the wall?

Recently I was in Bridgwater, Somerset, a town in the South West of England. Sitting in my car outside a school, I was chatting with the local Anglican vicar about young people and the Church. He told me about a recent incident involving a pupil from the school. As part of Religious Education, a group of 13-year-olds had visited his church. He was showing them around and explaining the significance of the various symbols but one boy kept tugging at his sleeve to get his attention. Eventually the vicar turned to him and asked what he wanted. The boy pointed up to a large crucifix hanging on the wall above their heads. 'Who's the bloke on the wall?' he asked.

It is hard to believe that in a town in England a boy of 13 could go into a church and not have the first idea of who Jesus is. As hard as it is to believe, it is true.

But it's not just young people who are ignorant about Jesus.

Crystal Carpets is in Essex and, as you might guess, it is a shop that sells carpets. A number of years ago my wife and I moved house and wanted a new carpet. It was a hot summer day and when we went to Crystal Carpets to buy one I was wearing shorts, a vest and my favourite shades. Having looked around for a while, and pulled our children out at least a hundred times from the tubes that the carpets are rolled onto, we found a carpet that we liked. I went over to the owner, a guy probably in his fifties, sitting at an old wooden desk in the middle of the shop. I asked him how he would like me to pay and he requested a deposit cheque and said I could pay the balance when the carpet was laid.

I wrote out the cheque and signed it in the appropriate place, just above my printed name, Reverend Dennis Pethers. I handed it to him and he took it, looked at it, looked at me then looked back at the cheque again before looking up once more at me.

It may have been the shades I was wearing, or perhaps the shorts and vest, but one thing was for sure, he didn't think I was a vicar.

As he stared into my face he said, 'You're not.'

'What?' I said.

He said it again: 'You're not.'

'What?' I asked again.

'You're not a vicar.' He continued, 'This isn't your cheque book, you've stolen it.'

I replied, 'No I haven't, I am a vicar, do you want me to prove it to you?'

He continued to look at me in disbelief as he slowly waved the cheque in the air. I couldn't think of what to say next, so I said, 'I'll say the Lord's Prayer if you like.'

Eventually I convinced him that I was in fact 'a vicar' and that it was my cheque book, I hadn't stolen it. I then had to stand alongside his desk while he filled in the paperwork. Whilst completing the various forms he kept looking up at me and shaking his head. What made it worse was that each time a new person walked into the shop he would look up and then point to me and ask them:

'What do you reckon he does for a living?'

Most people shrugged their shoulders looked bewildered and didn't answer him. A few made suggestions, the most memorable of which was 'Is he a second-hand car salesman?'

When he had finished the paperwork, there were no other people in the shop so he started talking to me about his own life. He told me that as a child he used to go to church three times every Sunday, but he stopped going because it was so boring and he was always getting told off. He still believed in God, still prayed, and he was glad that he had met somebody like me who had 'gone into the church'. He just didn't think church was for him, he wasn't religious enough! He continued to tell me that he hadn't bothered sending his own children to church because he didn't want them to have to suffer in the same way that he had!

There are countless stories that could be told about people across the

UK, people of different ages from different backgrounds but with one thing in common. They understand almost nothing about Jesus and never think about who He is or how He could change their lives.

Alongside ignorance of the truth about Jesus there is another challenge. These vast numbers of unreached people already have a view about the Church. They may have been forced to go as children or, as is increasingly the case, they may never have been at all, but somehow they have decided that it is not for them. They instinctively consider it to be old fashioned and irrelevant to their lives. This may not be an informed decision but nevertheless it often means that people never even begin to think about Jesus because they don't want to go to church and become religious.

They've left because they've got the message

Speaking at a luncheon on Merseyside, I was outlining the contribution the Church makes in society. A number of key people from the local community were there, including the headmaster of a secondary school. Over lunch, after I had spoken, he thanked me for what I had said and then offered his view regarding the Church: 'I don't think you will ever attract people back to church because they have got the message that they are not really wanted.'

I quizzed him further. He continued, 'Well you have to know how to behave if you are going to go to church, and most people don't – it just puts them off.'

If the headmaster is right, and I think he is, then it seems clear that most people in the UK do not consider church to have any place in their lives at all. If they think about church at all they think of it as being for religious people – and they are not religious.

It's tragic to think that a young boy in Somerset can go into a church and have to ask 'Who's the bloke on the wall?' because he has no idea of who Jesus is. Perhaps even more alarming is that most people in Britain will never even ask the question. As far as they are concerned, church is not for them; it is for religious people. As somebody once put it. 'People in church think they're better than the rest of us, and they're not.'

So our society has said no to church; that may depress us, or it could provide us with a great opportunity, an opportunity to help people today to see that faith in Jesus has positive results.

One of the guys in the tennis team I play in is called Ray. When I first met him we would just say 'Good evening' to each other, 'Well played' if one of us hit a good shot. One evening, after a match, I was sitting at the bar in our tennis club with Ray and we began to talk. He told me about his life, how his wife had left him, his boys had gone to live with her, he had lost his home, and how, on top of all of this, while he was going through all these things, his mother had died. He asked me about myself, so I talked about my family, my faith and my work. Once he had overcome his shock at finding out that I was what he called a vicar, we started to talk about God and life. Over the next half an hour or so he went into more depth about all that had happened to him. He seemed almost relieved to be able to talk about these things to somebody who would just listen to him.

As he talked I was able to say a little about certain things that had happened in my life and how at key moments my faith had been such a help. Ray didn't object to my talking about faith. In fact he said, 'I suppose you're right, there must be more to life than this.'

This surely is our starting point, faith in Jesus does bring 'more to life' – it is good news – but most people just haven't got it.

2

Who's the bloke on the street?

So just how bad is it? These stories are interesting, but how representative are they?

I think that the general feeling most of us have within the Church is that things are getting worse. Some of us may look back to the 'good old days' when the churches were full, with people of all ages, but now things are different. On the other hand, you may be at a church that is full and thriving but you are nonetheless aware that you are still only scratching the surface in terms of the number of people living in the town.

Numbers – helpful or not?

Much work has been done recently to discover just what is happening with regards to church attendance. The numbers present what seems to be a frightening reality. They speak of continual decline and when projected forward suggest that if things continue in the way they are, then the Church in the UK will cease to exist within a given number of years.

What is helpful about numbers is that they enable us to grasp the real situation. They cause us to face the fact that even if my church is full there is still much to be done.

What is unhelpful about them is that they can lead to some feeling depressed. There is nothing that can be done, decline is inevitable, so what's the point of trying to make a difference?

Rather than spending a lot of time looking at the precise figures, I think it is important to grasp the general trends and, more importantly, the implications of those trends. To make it easier to grasp I will take some inspiration from one of my favourite TV experiences. I am one of those sad people who, once every four years or so, stays up all night to watch the results of the general election. I love the drama as the results begin to come through and more than anything I love the part where they ask Peter Snow (the BBC election news presenter) what these results mean. As the camera locks in on him, you see him standing in front of the swingometer. With energy and enthusiasm he explains that if all the results follow the pattern of the ones received so far there will be a swing from one party to the other. At this point, behind him, the arrow on the swingometer swings and the computer-generated heads, representing seats, change from one colour to another. Meanwhile Peter, now with arms waving and with real excitement in his voice, tells the nation 'what this means'. It's great, I love it!

To help you grasp the trends of church attendance in the last century, imagine that the Church had commissioned a swingometer-reading to cover the whole of the twentieth century. Below is a very rough, but startling, picture of what we would discover.[1]

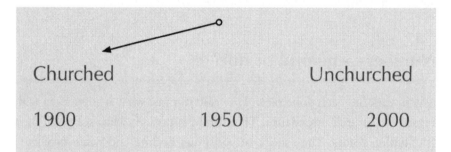

Figure 1 – The beginning of the twentieth century

At the beginning of the century:

- 83% of adults over 16 claimed to have attended Sunday school or Bible class for several years in their childhood.
- A further 11% had attended for a short time.
- Only 6% had never attended.

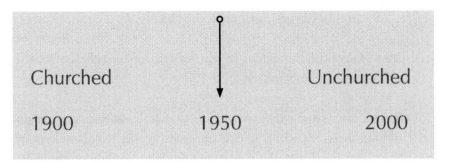

Figure 2 – The middle of the twentieth century

By the 1950s:

- 54% of English parents claimed that their children were currently attending Sunday school.

There is clear evidence of a downward trend. Parents are not all encouraging their children to do what they themselves had done.

While the downward trend can be seen between the 1930s and the 1950s it is still true to say that some 5 million English children were learning about Christ in the 1950s.

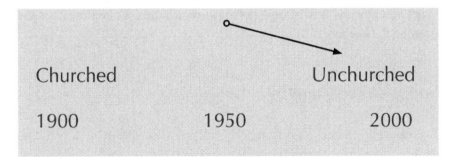

Figure 3 – The end of the twentieth century

By the time of the 1989 survey the downward trend had escalated remarkably.[2]

The 1989 English Church census revealed that:

- Only 14% of children under 15 years of age were in a church-related activity on a typical Sunday.

Different surveys and studies may come to slightly different conclusions on exact numbers but all agree that the trend in the twentieth century, which has continued into the twenty-first is that church attendance has continued to decline.

People not numbers

It seems the headmaster was right. People have got the message and in one century the Church has lost touch with 90% of its 'audience'. So how on earth do we ever get them back? It can't be just carrying on with what we do because clearly that has not worked.

So lots of people have stopped, or increasingly it is they have never started, the habit of going to church. If we are going to help them find out about Jesus it is just as important that we know something about them – who are these people that we want to share some good news with? How much do they know already? Is what they already know a help or a hindrance to them wanting to hear more?

Some consequences

The opening chapter of the report, entitled 'The Death of a National Custom', [3] begins with the following quotation:

> But equally there are large groups of traditionally 'Christian' countries who belong to the dominant majority community, yet know nothing of Christ. In some countries the old pattern of Sunday school has changed and religious education in schools has borne scant fruit, so that whole generations have grown up without a knowledge of the Bible. As societies

increasingly become secularised and technology focuses on the material realm, new generations drift into a world where Christianity has limited influence …

This exposes something very important: as the influences on people have changed so have their assumptions. It is worth looking at this in a little more depth.

Influences have changed

As fewer people have been attending church on a regular basis so the influence of the Church has declined. This has been seen in Figures 1–3. Alongside the declining influence of the Church has been the declining influence of parents.

Gerald Priestland describes the generations that began to drift away from church as 'The great Church of the unchurched'. For him, this description best describes a generation that believed in God, prayed fairly frequently and believed they should live by a broadly Christian moral code. This 'Church of the unchurched' grew as parents felt less inclined to attend church themselves and became less interested in passing the faith onto their children.

Increasingly, the great Church of the unchurched has itself diminished and now the most fitting description is simply 'unchurched'.

In place of these traditional influences two new influences emerged during the twentieth century. The rise of the electronic media has been, and continues to be, a hugely powerful influence upon people and, aligned with the media, the influence of friends or peers has largely reinforced its message.

These changes in influence are simply demonstrated below in Figures 4 and 5.

Three greatest influences:
• Parents
• Church
• School

Three greatest influences:
• Media
• Friends
• School

Figure 4 – 1950s child   Figure 5 – 2000s child

The result of these changing influences is that the Christian message is largely ignored. The report contains a depressing paragraph outlining the extent of the demise of the Church's influence:

> The outworking of present strategies is that England is nearing the end of a de-Christianising process. As Philip Cliff suggests in *The Rise and Development of the Sunday School Movement*, 'it takes only two generations to de-Christianise a people'.
>
> We are now seeing children born to the second generation of non-Sunday school parents. We may have improved our strategy to introduce children to Christ and His Church but vastly fewer children are within our reach. We have rightly been exercised in establishing the proper place for the child in God's Church, but in the process of so doing we have lost contact with the vast majority of the children in God's world.[4]

Not just children

While many of the numbers above relate to children it is crucial to bear in mind that many of those who were children at the time of the surveys are now adults and have children and even grandchildren of their own. These parents and grandparents have little or no awareness of church and unfortunately for many that do the experience is one that they would rather forget!

Assumptions have changed

These new influences have combined to create a whole new set of assumptions.

But how does watching TV, for example, alter people's assumptions as to what life is all about?

The trickle down effect

The result of these new influences is that the vast majority of people now have a whole new set of assumptions. How has this happened? One of the great Christian thinkers of our day is Ravi Zacharias. In his excellent book, *Can Man Live Without God?*,[5] he refers to the 'trickle down effect' as the process whereby people's assumptions are formed. He describes three levels of influence on individuals within society. I will use his model to explore how 'the bloke on the street' has vastly different assumptions now to those he would have had at the beginning of the twentieth century.

Level 1 – Foundational – Theory

Please don't lose interest at this point. It is very tempting to look at words like 'foundational' and 'theory' and think that now it all gets complicated and academic. But please hang on in there.

The foundational level is the level of logic and sound reasoning. It is what takes place in universities and colleges. Academics consider the big questions and present their various arguments. As we will see soon, these views trickle down and form the assumptions of 'the bloke on the street'. But before we consider that, it is important to look at some of the major foundational 'truths' that have become dominant in the past 100 years or so.

Existentialism: During the twentieth century, a new way of understanding life began to be formed at foundational level. Jean-Paul Sartre (1905–1980) introduced and developed a view of life that became known as 'existentialism'. This sounds complicated but actually expresses a fairly simple idea: 'You exist first and then find out what the essence of life is.' Simply, existentialism is a view that there is no ready-made meaning in life, no inbuilt or 'God-given' purpose. Individuals exist and by their own free choices and deliberate actions create their own meaning in life.

As such, existentialism removes God as both the source of life and the One who determines how life should be lived. The removal of God as the Creator dispenses with the idea of people as creatures, and those who exist are not subject to any higher authority than themselves. Each person is totally free to make his or her own meaning and this 'meaning' can only be determined by each individual him or herself.

This view of life that dispensed with God has developed further in recent decades with the emergence of what has become known as postmodernism.

Postmodernism. Gene Edward Veith helpfully defines how this new understanding of life is a development of existentialism.

> The postmodernist ideology is more than simple relativism. Whereas modern existentialism teaches that meaning is created by the individual, postmodern existentialism teaches that meaning is created by a social group and its language. According to this view, personal identity and the very contents of one's thoughts are all social constructions. The old existentialism stressed the alienated individual, dignified in loneliness and nonconformity; postmodern existentialism stresses social identity, group think, and fashion sense. Postmodern existentialism goes back to Nietzsche to emphasise not only will, but power. Liberation comes from rebelling against existing power structures, including oppressive notions of 'knowledge' and 'truth'.[6]

There is so much in this comment from Veith, but again it is not as complicated as it may appear. Simply, postmodernism suggests that meaning in life is not found when an individual 'does what he is told'. In that sense while it is like existentialism it differs because it does not see meaning in life being achieved by the individual just 'doing what he wants'. The key emphasis of postmodernism is that meaning in life is found by belonging to a group and that belonging to this group opposes any notion of power. No other group has the authority to say that the behaviour or beliefs of the group the individual has chosen to belong to are wrong.

Existentialism disposed of any idea of there being a God, postmodernism disposes of any idea that there is any one group that has the truth. So, Christianity cannot be the truth, but like any claim to being the truth, it is nothing more than a world-view that has been constructed in order to control and oppress others. It is worth saying that postmodernism is not anti religious, it considers 'science' also to be a 'constructed truth'. The key point is that for postmodernists there is no one foundational truth, any such claims are mere fiction.

Most people do not consider themselves to be either existentialists or postmodernists. They probably have never heard the words let alone know what they mean and they have not made a conscious decision to become existentialists. However, these foundational ideas have been powerfully communicated to the vast majority of people through the best possible vehicle for communication – the electronic media.

Level 2 – Influential – the media

Never before has there been a time when people can be influenced so quickly, so powerfully and so chaotically. Ravi Zacharias cites the electronic media as the vehicle that influences individuals within society. He states:

Through technology the whole world has now become the media's parish, talk show hosts the prophets, actors and musicians the priests, and any script will do for the Scriptures as long as moral constraints are removed. Sitting before a well-lit box is all the cultic performance needs, and each person can enthrone his or her own self as divine. Truth has been relegated to subjectivity; beauty has been subjugated to the beholder;

and as millions are idiotized night after night, a global commune has been constructed with the arts enjoying a totalitarian rule.[7]

The global impact of media is unprecedented, foundational ideas are popularised and communicated through media to vast numbers of people across the world. Of course the media does not invite people to become existentialists or postmodernists, but it powerfully and persuasively communicates the underlying principles of these ideas in such a way that the mass audiences accept that these are the important things in life.

Colin Morris in his book *God in a Box* outlines how powerfully the television communicates its message: 'Television is not in the business of offering an escapist alternative to the real world. Where television is, there is the real world. The medium has the ability to impose its view of reality on everyone who comes within the range of its signals ...'[8]

He continues:

For the first time in five hundred years, the word is no longer the dominant force in shaping our culture. The atmosphere flashes with the rich imagery of television. This does not mean that words have stopped being important, but they do not predominate.

The image, chiefly projected through the television screen, is now the most powerful way of transmitting our culture.[9]

It is the image that has become dominant in what Morris calls 'transmitting our culture'. This is the perfect vehicle for communicating a view of life that finds meaning by 'doing your own thing', which in most cases means being part of a group that follows a certain fashion, style of music or behaviour. The electronic media powerfully presents its images to a mass audience, leaving individuals to choose for themselves what they want to believe, and which group they want to be part of.

Colin Morris quotes Harvey Cox, a US theologian, and refers to the emergence in society of 'post literate' man. He continues: 'The age of writing is over ... The visual electronic image has replaced the written word as the crucial unit of communication ... As the post-literate person evolves, his or her world view will differ radically from that of the age of writing.'[10]

The report 'All God's Children?' was not blind to the power of the media in shaping the views of children and young people. It contained the following quotations:

> The world of our children is virtually controlled by the media – which portrays a more exciting world than the real one. Everything is highly coloured, fast, slick, more professional and sophisticated, so that family, home and school can seem boring by contrast. (Pat Wynne Jones) [11]

> Most of the stories, told to most of the children … are not told by the parents, not by the schools, not by the Church, but by a small group of distant corporations. (Professor George Gerbner) [12]

These quotations are so telling. They speak of new generations of children who will not listen to stories told by their parents. These stories are being replaced by images given, not by those who are concerned for their development, but by those who will never meet them. It is these 'stories' that have been influencing children, young people and adults for generations now. And the impact of this influence on the man on the street is seen at Level 3, the conversational level.

Level 3 – Conversational

It is here, in the ordinary, everyday lives of people that the effect of the media's powerful influence in communicating the foundational ideas can be seen. There are two areas where the assumptions of the man on the street can be seen to have changed so much from the time when the Church was the dominant influence.

Values

The moral framework that guides the decisions that people make, or their values, has changed enormously.

I will always remember taking a lesson in a school and asking young people of around 15 if they knew the Ten Commandments. Some young people had called out a few and we had two or three on the projector screen. One lad had his arm raised so high that it was almost coming out of its socket. Eventually I said, 'OK, tell me a commandment.' The other 150 or so young people in the class all looked at him, and he gave his answer.

'If you can't think of anything nice to say don't say anything at all.'

Everybody looked at him and then looked at me. 'Is he right?' was etched across their faces.

I looked back at him and then said, 'I'm afraid that's not a commandment … it's what Thumper said in the Disney film *Bambi*.'

The class erupted in laughter and the poor lad went redder than I have ever seen anybody go before or since.

Each time I took this lesson we would manage eventually, with a lot of help, to get all ten commandments up on the screen. I would always write them in modern English, no thees and thous! I would then ask the young people what they thought the commandments have become today. Here are just a few things they have said:

'Steal things but don't get caught.'

'Commit adultery unless he is bigger than you or can run faster.'

'Me first not God first.'

One lad didn't come up with a suggestion, he couldn't understand one of the commandments at all. He asked, 'Is adultery getting old?' He couldn't understand why God commanded people not to get old, how could God punish you for that, you couldn't help it!

A similar rejection of traditional Christian values is just as evident amongst adults. In fact I have observed that many young people are becoming disappointed with their parents' values!

There is a humorous side to these stories and I confess that I have often been amused by the answers and views given. But there is something vital that must be taken from all of this. The idea of there being a 'right' way and a 'wrong' way to live is no longer the dominant view. This has been replaced by something like, 'If it feels good or makes me happy then it must be right.' This is existentialism! Many people today have little or no awareness or understanding of 'sin'. If there is no right or wrong way to live then the idea of sin is irrelevant. Put another way: if everybody can live how they like and there are no consequences, then the message of Jesus seems to have little to say.

This move from the way of living that God outlined in the Bible, to people being free to do their own thing, is not the only thing that has changed. Values have changed out of all recognition, but so have beliefs.

Beliefs

I think that the most insightful summary of the beliefs of people in the twenty-first century was given a number of years before by G.K. Chesterton when he said: 'When people stop believing in God, they don't believe in nothing, they believe in anything.'

This statement so accurately reflects where many are today – totally confused. Most people I meet are not convinced atheists (opposed to the idea that God exists). Nor are they thoughtful agnostics (not convinced either way). I think we need a new term. My term is not as grand sounding as these two, and it is not even mine. I have stolen it from one of the young people attending a training session I ran. I asked the group which word best summed up people's beliefs today, and Becky said 'muddled'. I can't think of a better word, most people just don't know what they believe and so they are left in a state of confusion.

The challenge we face is that the Church has been marginalised. Christian beliefs are no longer 'assumed' to be true; in addition, the way we communicate what we believe is outdated. The combination of these two things is that church is no longer in the 'mainstream' of people's lives, it is on the edge of things, and now largely ignored by 'the bloke on the street'. Someone who helped me greatly in my early days was an evangelist called Vic Jacopson, I remember hearing him tell a story once that illustrated this perfectly.

Vic spoke of going on a family visit to the zoo, and the excitement that his family felt as the time approached for 'Penguin Feeding Time'. They stood against the barrier as the penguins were fed. Great buckets of fish were emptied as the zoo keepers threw the fish into the water and the penguins went crazy, diving, swimming, splashing, squabbling over the fish; darting, ducking, all at great speed, to catch as many fish as they could. Vic told us that, as he watched this scene, he glanced over to the edge of the pool where all the activity was taking place and there, on a rock, standing proud and erect was a huge penguin. Occasionally a fish would come his way, either a bad throw from the zoo keeper, or perhaps flipped into the air by one of the over-excited penguins. As the fish fell within its reach the penguin would bend over and quickly gobble it up. Then it would return to its original position, standing on the rock, erect and proud. I loved hearing Vic tell the story, he is a great storyteller, but the point behind it was so powerful. Jesus said we were to be 'fishers' of men. Most of the fish at penguin feeding time were being caught in the water, in the 'mainstream of life – where the action is', many of these were being gobbled up by other faiths, sects and philosophies. But there on the rock, erect and proud, was the Church. Not involved in 'the action' but, without moving, it could eat just enough fish to keep it alive!

It's far more exciting and dangerous in the water, and that's where Jesus wants us all to be! It's time to get off the rock, the rock that represents our customs and traditions and a bygone day when people came to us because they assumed it was the right thing to do. The moment we live in requires that don't just do what we've always done and hope things improve. It's time to go to them – now is our moment. But if we are to go, what are we going to say? What is the message of Jesus?

PART 2

The
Message

3

Jesus – the message is announced

As we saw in the last chapter, most people have not actively rejected Jesus, they have simply got the wrong message about Him. They think that faith in Jesus means 'becoming religious'. And in a world where religion is rejected, and doing your own thing is persuasively presented, new generations of people are not likely to begin coming to church.

This 'becoming religious' requires, they think, having to participate in a number of rituals that appear meaningless and outdated. In addition, many feel that 'religion' is for people who think they are better than everybody else, but who are not! So, many will say, 'I believe in God – but I'm not religious.' What they are expressing is that faith in God is possible without ritual and self-righteousness.

It is sad that the vast majority of people have got 'the message' that Jesus is for religious people – but was that His message?

The message of Jesus

I have included a simple model here that expresses how Jesus summarised His purpose in coming to the world, or His 'message': 'For the Son of Man came to seek and to save what was lost' (Luke 19:10).

Jesus came to actively look for, and save, lost people.

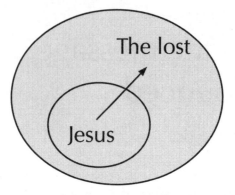

If the Church is to be faithful in communicating the message of Jesus it is key that what the Church does reveals this message rather than conceals it.

Who will enter the kingdom of God?

Key to the teaching of Jesus was this question. Another way of asking it is, 'Who will be saved?' or perhaps, 'Who will benefit from what Jesus accomplished?'

As we read the Gospels in the twenty-first century it is so easy to miss the potency of Jesus' message because we do not pay attention to the particular circumstances in which He said the things He said. We read them as 'Christians' and those that follow Him whereas much of what He taught was to people who were not yet His followers.

Much of what I want to say regarding Jesus' message will be taken from the chapters building up to Luke 19:10, but John, at the beginning of his Gospel, sets the scene perfectly:

He [Jesus] was in the world, and though the world was made through him, the world did not recognise him. He came to that which was his own, but his own did not receive him. Yet to all who received him, to those who believed in his name, he gave the right to be called children of God – children born not of natural descent, nor of human decision or a husband's will, but born of God. (John 1:10–13)

To us today, reading these words is an affirmation of what we already know, but to the original readers these words were nothing short of revolutionary. John was introducing a theme that is rampant throughout his and indeed each of the Gospels. This is the surprising fact that Jesus has come for the very people that those who called themselves 'God's people' excluded. When John wrote '… his own did not receive him' he was referring to the Jews – 'God's chosen people'. It is hard for us living today to grasp the immense significance of these few words. These people, God's people, did not receive Jesus but rejected Him. What follows would have been even more remarkable to the first readers of this Gospel: 'Yet to all who received him, to those who believed in his name, he gave the right to be called children of God …' This verse demonstrates that, contrary to all that people thought at this time, becoming a child of God was not something that was achieved by birthright and following traditions, but something that happened on God's initiative as a consequence of 'receiving Jesus and believing in his name'.

John was introducing the astounding fact that the good news wasn't for religious people, it was for sinners!

This theme is central to the message that Jesus communicated. Repeatedly He makes it clear that relationship with God and belonging to the community of 'believers' is not 'earned' by virtue of birthright. Jesus taught that relationship with God follows an encounter with Him that leads to a change of heart.

Good news

Jesus' message is often referred to as the gospel, or the good news. The Greek word that we translate is *Euaggelion*. The *Eu* part means 'good/pleasant', the *aggelion* (pronounced 'angelion') means message. It is the word used to describe angels who are messengers of God. Thus Jesus' message was a good message – it had something of real benefit and those who were to benefit were those who least deserved it – sinners!

Despite the fact that this news was good, the religious people of His day didn't like Jesus' message; they didn't want this gift – in their opinion they already knew God, they were descendants of Abraham and that, along with their observance of the law, was all they needed. The religious leaders, far from receiving the good news gladly, opposed Jesus and sought to undermine Him and have Him removed. It is this conflict regarding the basis on which people can know God that provides the context for so much of what Jesus said. And it is this conflict that is the key issue in the chapters leading up to Jesus' great announcement in Luke 19:10.

Luke, like all of the evangelists when they wrote their record of the 'good news' or gospel, did not just write a list of events about Jesus as a memoir of His existence. They wanted to make a point, to provoke a response in those who would read the good news. Consequently, it is often helpful not just to read stories in the Gospels in isolation, but to see them as part of the whole: where do they fit, what comes before and what comes after? What was the crux of the message that Luke was passing on to his readers?

The chunk of Luke that I want to consider begins at chapter 14 verse 1 and ends with Jesus' declaration in chapter 19 verse 10: 'For the Son of Man came to seek and to save what was lost.'

In chapter 14, Luke records an occasion that sets the scene for what will follow. Jesus, while He was at the house of a Pharisee, healed a man suffering from dropsy (14:1–14). This incident, Luke records, took place on the Sabbath, and it provided Jesus with the opportunity to tell the religious leaders that it is better to rescue, save, heal, restore on the Sabbath, than observe Sabbath law and let people perish. Later in the meal Jesus reminded those listening that it is fitting to be humble not arrogant when invited to a party, 'For everyone who exalts himself will be humbled, and he who humbles himself will be exalted' (14:11). Jesus clearly pointed out that God invites the humble who need His mercy, not the proud who think they have the right to come because they keep the law. Being part of the community of faith is not for those who think they are 'righteous'. It is not those who exalt themselves who will inherit the kingdom, but those who are humble. Matthew records Jesus saying, 'Blessed are the poor in spirit [the humble not the proud], for theirs is the kingdom of heaven' (Matt. 5:3).

So the scene is set. Jesus has opened a proverbial can of worms. And now He states, in no uncertain terms, that the way to God is not, as religious people think, by observing customs and keeping the law. It is because of Jesus, and only because of Jesus, that people can come to God.

The parable of the great banquet (Luke 14:15–24) is in response to a guest at the house of the Pharisee saying, 'Blessed is the man who will eat at the feast in the kingdom of God' (14:15). Jesus took this opportunity to explore 'who will eat at this feast' or 'who will enter the kingdom of God'. The parable makes it clear that those who had been invited, clearly the Jews, 'his own who did not receive him' (John 1:11), do not respond to the invitation, so the owner of the house, clearly God, invites everybody else. In the parable Jesus is at pains to point out that God invites the least likely people to the 'feast in the kingdom of God' and concludes by saying that not one of those who were invited (and didn't respond) will get a taste of it. Harsh words indeed, I'm sure they didn't make Jesus a popular 'party' guest. But this is just the beginning.

In 15:1–2, Luke records: 'Now the tax collectors and "sinners" were all gathering round to hear him. But the Pharisees and the teachers of the law muttered, "This man welcomes sinners, and eats with them." '

This verse is key, it is an introduction not just to the parable of the lost sheep which begins in verse 3 but to a series of parables, including the lost coin (vv.8–10), and the lost son (vv.11–32). Indeed Howard Marshall suggests that this phrase '… is perhaps meant to indicate that the general circumstances of Jesus' ministry rather than one particular incident are in mind'.[1]

It is this conflict between the Jewish leaders and Jesus' message that He had come for sinners that is always present in Jesus' teaching. This seems to be the case because, although these three parables are clearly addressed to the Pharisees and the 'sinners', it does not end after the parable of the lost son, it continues beyond that; but we will look at these three parables first.

Three parables – one message

Each of these three parables follows a similar pattern. Something of real value is lost, then found, and the result is a celebration or party. I have often heard sermons on these parables and the main message has been to remind everybody in the church of how special each of us is to God. While I do not deny that this is true, and that these parables do say this, that is not the main purpose. There is something even deeper. Jesus is stating that all people, however bad (remember there are 'sinners' listening), are loved by God, but the problem with those who call themselves religious and say that they love God (remember there are Pharisees listening), is that they think that they earn and deserve God's favour.

These parables are unbridled onslaughts on the attitude of those who thought of themselves as righteous and deserving of God's favour and, at the same time, wonderful pictures that expose God's great compassion and desire for those who are lost.

Let's look at them.

The first is a direct attack on the Pharisees.

The Lost Sheep, Luke 15:1–7 In this parable the owner of 100 sheep desperately seeks one that is lost and celebrates with his friends and neighbours when it is found.

William Hendriksen writes: 'In order to expose the terrible mistake the Pharisees, etc., were making and the horrible wrong they were committing, and at the same time to convince them of this, that even now they might turn from their wicked attitude toward those who were in need of compassion and help, Jesus tells this parable.' [2]

It is no coincidence that it happened to be a sheep that was lost. The religious leaders who were listening to Jesus' words knew that God often referred to His people as sheep and to the leaders as shepherds. Ezekiel writes, 'I myself will tend my sheep and make them lie down, declares the Sovereign LORD. I will search for the lost and bring back the strays' (Ezek. 34:15–16).

Ezekiel paints the picture of a compassionate God who searches for the lost. But God's attitude of compassion and mercy in these verses is in stark contrast to the leaders of God's people at the time of Ezekiel. Earlier in chapter 34 Ezekiel was commissioned by God to speak hard words to the religious leaders (the shepherds). 'The word of the LORD came to me: "Son of man, prophesy against the shepherds of Israel; prophesy and say to them: 'This is what the Sovereign LORD says: Woe to the shepherds of Israel who only take care of themselves! Should not shepherds take care of the flock'"?' (34:1–2).

It seems likely that these verses from Ezekiel were in Jesus' mind as He told this parable. He is drawing a contrast between God's compassion for the lost and the shepherds who only take care of themselves. This failure of the shepherds in Ezekiel's time is the same as that of the leaders of God's people that Jesus was speaking against here.

Jesus concludes the parable with severe words, 'I tell you that in the same way there will be more rejoicing in heaven over one sinner who repents than over ninety-nine righteous persons who do not need to repent' (Luke 15:7).

William Hendriksen comments:

> In harmony with several other interpreters I am convinced that the meaning of verse 7 is, 'I tell you that similarly God … will rejoice over one sinner who becomes converted, and not over ninety-nine self righteous people.' Undoubtedly, in mentioning the ninety-nine, Jesus was thinking of the Pharisees, scribes and their followers. [3]

Jesus' final accusation is that these religious leaders are not the ones who cause God to rejoice. It is the sinner. The kingdom of God, Jesus is saying, is not for those who call themselves righteous. It is for those who admit they are lost and ask to be forgiven.

The next parable is also about something of value that has been lost – this time a coin.

The Lost Coin, Luke 15:8–10 In this parable the coin represents the sinner and is something very precious. As in the previous parable something is lost, then found and the result is a party. Surely the heart of this parable is that sinners are so precious to God that a party is thrown to celebrate when even one is found. Heaven celebrates but the Pharisees in contrast don't. They failed to see just how precious sinners were to God; they were too interested in taking care of themselves.

It is this failure on the part of the Pharisees, their failure to understand God's heart for lost people, that is hinted at here, but clearly portrayed in the next parable.

The Lost Son, Luke 15:11–32 It is this parable that most vividly shows the contrast between the 'joy in heaven' over the forgiven sinner, and the 'muttering and discontent' of those who think the kingdom is theirs because of their own righteousness.

The story *is* about God's grace and delight in sinners responding, but the 'amazingness' of this grace is seen in even more wonder when we consider the context and real purpose of the story. This 'grace' of God is in contrast to the 'grumbling' of the self-righteous religious leaders who think the inheritance is theirs by right.

This parable follows the same pattern as the previous two. The son is lost, found and then there is a party. But there is a dimension to this parable that is often sidelined when, in fact, I believe it is its main purpose.

It is often thought that the story is about two main characters and a minor one who comes in at the end and tries to spoil things a little. But there are three main characters.

Firstly, there is the son who becomes lost. There cannot be many things more precious than a son; this one though is not good, he gains then wastes his inheritance. He represents the 'sinners' – clearly he is not deserving of forgiveness, he is greedy, wasteful and reckless.

Then there is the father, who represents God. And last, but certainly not least, is the older brother. This brother clearly represents the muttering Pharisees and teachers of the law that Luke had referred to in chapter 15 verse 2.

And so to the story.

The father has two sons, the elder is a faithful son, the younger is altogether different. Jesus tells of how the younger took his share of the father's estate, moved away to a distant country and squandered everything. As a result of his wild living, and a famine, he reached desperation point – so desperate that he took a job feeding pigs. This for him as a Jew represented utter humiliation; pigs were regarded as unclean animals and Jesus, in this story, wanted to make it clear that things had got about as low as they could get for this young man.

It is important to remember that this mess was of his own making, he couldn't blame anybody else. As a result, he could not earn his way back into his father's favour, all he could do was ask for mercy. As he considers going back to his father he comes to his senses, 'I will set out and go back to my father and say to him: Father, I have sinned against heaven and against you. I am no longer worthy to be called your son; make me like one of your hired men' (vv.18–19).

Now we see the attitude of the father. As the 'sinner' returns, Jesus paints a beautiful picture that exposes God's great compassion for the lost: 'But while he was still a long way off, his father saw him and was filled with compassion for him; he ran to his son, threw his arms around him and kissed him' (v.20).

The father took the initiative, and ran to meet his undeserving son who, as he was being welcomed, blurted out, 'Father, I have sinned against heaven and against you. I am no longer worthy to be called your son.' But look at how the father responded. He did not condemn or blame his son; instead he threw a party. As with the shepherd who found the lost sheep and the woman who found her lost coin, so this delighted father threw the best of all parties to celebrate.

This sinner was welcome at the feast, but not as a 'sinner', because he was fully restored. Jesus tells how he was draped in the best robe, and that a ruby ring was put upon his finger; he had sandals for his feet and the best meat was put on the table. The kingdom of God is for those who are lost and when they are found it is time for celebration!

That is the story that is known and loved but it is only a part of the whole. If we are to really understand what Jesus was saying we must consider the other son. In some ways all the story so far is only an introduction to the main point of what Jesus was saying.

It is the elder son that this was really all about. He represented the grumbling Pharisees listening to this parable. Luke tells us they muttered because Jesus 'welcomes sinners and eats with them' (15:2) and now in this story Jesus talks of someone who will not eat with a sinner. Instead of rejoicing over the lost 'sinner' being found, he complained to the father that he had always done the right thing but never had even so much as a goat let alone the fatted calf. He did not rejoice in the 'salvation' of his brother because he didn't think it was fair that the father should forgive the 'sinner' rather than reward his 'righteousness'.

The story of the two brothers is a superb climax to this triplet of parables – it is those who seek mercy not those who think they deserve it who will enter the kingdom of God.

In case these parables aren't enough, Luke turns up the heat even more as he continues with this theme. Luke 17:11 points out that Jesus is now on His way to Jerusalem – this for Luke is the journey that will lead to Jesus' death and resurrection. Luke records some more incidents, sayings and parables of Jesus that explore this theme: 'Who will enter the kingdom of heaven and how?'

I want to take a look at some of the major parables and events that drive this theme home.

The Parable of the Pharisee and the Tax Collector, Luke 18:9–14

There can be nothing more direct than the parable of the Pharisee and the tax collector.

It is almost impossible for us to imagine or feel the impact this story would have had when Jesus first told it. Luke provides his explanation of why Jesus told the parable. 'To some who were confident of their own righteousness and looked down on everybody else, Jesus told this parable' (18:9). Those 'confident of their own righteousness' are clearly the Pharisees and religious leaders mentioned in 15:2 who muttered against Jesus associating with 'tax collectors' and sinners. Luke is continuing the same theme.

The story is pointed, deliberate and defiant. If there had been any doubt before, the religious leaders are left in none now as to Jesus' intention. They have misunderstood God's grace and, even more than that, have misled the people they were supposed to be caring for. They had become a barrier to God not a bridge.

In this story Jesus no longer uses sheep, rings or sons to represent the heart of His message. He dispenses with that and tells a story that is so clear in its message that it cannot be misunderstood.

The story is about the very people who are listening to Him, a Pharisee – one confident of his own righteousness – and a tax collector – clearly a person who more than anybody else was thought not to be deserving of entry into the kingdom of God. Jesus begins the story, 'Two men went up to the temple to pray, one a Pharisee and the other a tax collector' (18:10).

I must admit that I sometimes wonder how Jesus ever got to the end of this story without being attacked and killed there and then. Remember He was talking to Pharisees, and look at how He described the Pharisee. 'The Pharisee stood up and prayed about [or perhaps a better translation is "to"] himself.'

Clearly the Pharisee considered himself worthy to be in the presence of God – his prayer was like a spiritual CV that should get him the top job in the kingdom of God; but the tax collector, Luke tells us, '… stood at a distance. He would not even look up to heaven, but beat his breast and said, "God, have mercy on me, a sinner" ' (18:13).

This story, like the others, once again vividly presents the contrast. The tax collector who stood at a distance (I immediately think of the son who came home to his father and while he was still 'a long way off' the father ran to him) and the Pharisee who stood right at the front, in the presence of God.

The tax collector appealed to God's mercy and the Pharisee told God how good he, the Pharisee, was at keeping the commandments.

The conclusion of the story is that the one who sought mercy, the sinning tax collector, and not the self-righteous Pharisee, was justified before God. And then, once again, Jesus underlined, as He had at the Pharisee's house in chapter 14, that it is the humble, not the arrogant, who will enter the kingdom of God.

I am fascinated by what then unfolds in Luke. Just when you might think that it could not be made more obvious, things really begin to build up to a crescendo. Three more incidents that Luke records are worth looking at.

The Rich Ruler (Luke 18:18–29) This is the story of a rich man who asked Jesus what he must do to inherit eternal life. He had kept the law since he was a boy but Jesus told him that he still lacked one thing. He needed to follow Jesus and seek treasure in heaven rather than on earth. I have always been astounded by the brief dialogue between Jesus and this rich man which concludes with Jesus saying: 'You still lack one thing. Sell everything you have and give to the poor, and you will have treasure in heaven. Then come, follow me' (v.22). The next verse really hits home: 'When he heard this, he became very sad, because he was a man of great wealth' (v.23).

He will not enter the kingdom of God because what he has matters more than what he could have.

The Blind Beggar (Luke 18:35–43) Soon after is the story of a blind beggar who when he called out for mercy was rebuked by those around Jesus – they told him to be quiet. But in spite of their protests Jesus ordered the man to be brought to Him, then asked him, 'What do you want me to do for you?' Jesus granted his request and gave him his sight.

I am fascinated by this section of Luke because it includes stories and incidents concerning a tax collector, a rich man and a beggar who the crowds try to turn away from Jesus. Then, straight afterwards, Luke includes the incident regarding Zacchaeus, a tax collector who was rich, and who could not get to Jesus because of the crowds!

It is as if all that Jesus has been saying since chapter 14 was now going to be lived out in front of the Pharisees and 'sinners'. The Zacchaeus incident provides a perfect climax to all that has gone before and it provides Jesus with the opportunity to utter a sentence that summarises it all.

Zacchaeus the Tax Collector (Luke 19:1–10) It is likely that you are familiar with this story. If so, perhaps the most helpful thing to do to grasp the impact of this incident is to try to imagine some of the cute pictures of Zacchaeus that you may have coloured in if you were in Sunday school. Then take out an imaginary eraser and rub out the cute picture. Now pick up an imaginary pen or pencil and draw a different picture on the paper. Draw a picture of the person you find it most difficult to like and perhaps find it almost impossible to believe will be in heaven – you might not even want him or her to be there! Now look at this picture – this is how people viewed Zacchaeus, he was not a cute little man – he was hated!

This story perfectly demonstrates the heartbeat of the message of Jesus. It demonstrates why He came and for whom He came. Zacchaeus was the embodiment of a sinner. But he wanted to be changed. This led him to doing the undignified thing of chasing after Jesus and even climbing a tree in order to see Him. Again the contrast is seen as Jesus, who welcomed Zacchaeus, was accused of associating with sinners. But as a result of his encounter with Jesus, Zacchaeus was transformed, his heart was changed, he stopped being greedy and self-seeking and instead wanted to help others and bless those he had harmed.

The good news for sinners is that they can be changed, not into self-righteous people, but into kind and generous people. Zacchaeus did not enter the kingdom because he gave away his money, he was moved to give away his money because now he had a new heart and wanted to repair the damage he had done.

This story provides the climax to all that Luke has included since chapter 14. I have to say that I can never read this verse without feeling a tingle go down my spine:

'For the Son of Man came to seek and to save what was lost.'

The only hope for people is the Son of Man – He has come to demonstrate God's mercy. Nobody will be saved by their own 'righteousness' but by the transforming love of God.

It seems abundantly clear that the message of Jesus is that the kingdom of God is for those who seek mercy, not those who trust in their own righteousness and observance of the law. God has made it possible for people to know Him, but it is only because of Jesus, not because of any righteousness of our own.

The crucial role that Jesus had to play in enabling people to come to know God is hinted at right in the middle of these stories. Luke records, 'Jesus took the Twelve aside and told them, "We are going up to Jerusalem, and everything that is written by the prophets about the Son of Man will be fulfilled. He will be turned over to the Gentiles. They will mock him, insult him, spit on him, flog him and kill him. On the third day he will rise again"' (18:31–33).

The importance of Jesus' death and resurrection was not revealed to the disciples at this time, but later they came to understand that God could show mercy to sinners. Matthew recorded, interestingly again in the context of humility and not pride, that Jesus said, '… the Son of Man did not come to be served, but to serve, and to give his life as a ransom for many' (Matt. 20:28).

The message of Jesus was clearly that salvation is a gift that has been paid for, at the expense of His life, it cannot be earned!

4

The apostles –
the message is revealed

J esus had lived and died to communicate the message that God has a desire and passion to find lost sinners. Following His resurrection, Jesus entrusted this message to those who had been with Him throughout His ministry. All that He had accomplished on behalf of humanity was entrusted to His followers; they were to tell the world.

So what did Jesus' followers do with His message once He had gone? He told them to go and they went – but what happened as they went?

The message communicated by the first disciples

Following Jesus' resurrection, John tells us in his Gospel:

> On the evening of that first day of the week, when the disciples were together, with the doors locked for fear of the Jews, Jesus came and stood among them and said, 'Peace be with you!' After he said this, he showed them his hands and side. The disciples were overjoyed when they saw the Lord. Again Jesus said, 'Peace be with you! As the Father has sent me, I am sending you.' (John 20:19–21)

Matthew records,

> 'All authority in heaven and on earth has been given to me. Therefore go and make disciples of all nations, baptising them in the name of the Father and of the Son and of the Holy Spirit, and teaching them to obey everything I have commanded you. And surely I am with you always, to the very end of the age.' (Matt. 28:18–20)

These accounts clearly demonstrate that Jesus sent His disciples into the world to continue to do what He had done; their message was His message, their task was to tell the world His message. This message is the same one that we must share today, but what was Jesus' message and how faithful were His first disciples in communicating it rather than their own?

In the book of Acts, Luke records: '... you will receive power when the Holy Spirit comes on you; and you will be my witnesses in Jerusalem, and in all Judea and Samaria, and to the ends of the earth' (Acts 1:8).

Jesus' command here, as in Matthew's Gospel, was to take His message to the whole world. The disciples were to be 'witnesses' of all they had seen and experienced and come to know of Jesus. They would be going beyond the geographical boundaries of Jerusalem and Judea, beyond Samaria, into all the world.

This 'going beyond' Jerusalem meant that the early disciples would have two 'distances' to travel. The first is the obvious one: the geographical distance. They covered thousands of miles travelling from place to place. This was challenging and exhausting but it was not the greatest challenge. The greater challenge was less obvious; it was the world-view or philosophical distance. As they travelled the miles to new towns, cities and nations they found that the people they came into contact with had vastly different views and assumptions about truth, life, faith and the character of God. The further they travelled from Jerusalem, so the people were less and less familiar with the Jewish faith, with all of its laws and customs. The challenge and opportunity for these disciples would be to express Jesus' message in such a way that it would make sense to people who were not familiar with the Jewish faith and its law and customs

Backhouse and Tylor provide a useful introduction to the world that the early disciples were sent into: '... The Jewish people were in expectation of the advent of the Messiah, the Gentile nations, awakening to the consciousness that their idols were no gods and their philosophy vain, were panting for something higher and more satisfying.' [1]

It was to such a world, a melting pot of ideas and beliefs awaiting a truth that would draw the strands together, that the 'good news' was communicated and in which it spread rapidly.

Jerusalem and the Jews

The disciples were told to begin in Jerusalem and they did exactly that. Acts 2:1–47 records the beginnings of the Church there. This is a riveting account of how the first church began as a result of Peter preaching to a vast crowd gathered in Jerusalem to celebrate the festival of Pentecost. Acts 2:5 states: 'Now there were staying in Jerusalem God-fearing Jews from every nation under heaven.' Miraculously, the Holy Spirit interpreted Peter's words so that all could understand. The result was that those gathered were 'cut to the heart' (2:37) and about 3,000 responded to the message. But what was his message?

Peter's preaching was very direct. He knew that those who were listening were God-fearing Jews, so he drew their attention to key themes that they would have understood and then demonstrated how these had been fulfilled in Jesus. Having done this he then directly confronted his hearers and accused them of failing to receive this Jesus, '… and you, with the help of wicked men, put him to death by nailing him to the cross' (v.23). But, in spite of their arrogance and wickedness God has fulfilled what He promised in Jesus, He raised Him from the dead. Peter continues, 'Therefore let all Israel be assured of this: God has made this Jesus, whom you crucified, both Lord and Christ' (v.36).

On hearing this, Luke records, the hearers were 'cut to the heart' and asked Peter and the other apostles, 'Brothers, what shall we do?' (v.37).

Peter's reply is that they need to repent and trust in God's mercy. This is true for them as it will be true for all people everywhere. This is a clear continuation of the message that Jesus preached. God gives grace to the humble and opposes the proud. What Jesus pointedly preached in the parable of the Pharisee and the tax collector is now being applied. The Jews listening to Peter were told they needed God's mercy just as much as anybody else. The good news he had for them was that Jesus had made that mercy possible because of His death and resurrection. It was Jesus and only Jesus who had made it possible for them to be saved.

Those who responded began to meet together and, Luke records, 'They devoted themselves to the apostles' teaching and to the fellowship, to the breaking of bread and to prayer' (2:42).

A new movement had begun, the first community of believers in Jesus was formed. Jesus' command to His disciples to be witnesses was being fulfilled and His promise to be with them was seen to be true. As Peter witnessed to Jesus, so Jesus, by the Holy Spirit, brought about transformation in the lives of those who heard.

Beyond Jerusalem

But, as Jesus had said, this good news was not just for those in Jerusalem – it had to be taken beyond. The first ten chapters of the book of Acts are all concerned with those who, while they were not Jewish, were nevertheless familiar with the law and customs of the Jewish faith.

As Michael Green points out: 'The preaching to Samaritans and pious proselytes like the Ethiopian Eunuch (8:26–39) and Cornelius (10:1–48), though remarkable enough in all conscience, could be regarded as an extension of the bounds of Israel to the "Strangers within the gate". Not so the preaching to sheer pagans, which began, we are told, in Antioch.' [2]

The good news that was communicated to people who valued Jewish customs was, that these customs and their observance of the law could not save them, salvation was only possible through faith in Christ. This was what Jesus had taught and His followers continued to teach the same thing.

But as the gospel spread farther away from Jerusalem, it was communicated to people who didn't value these customs in the same way, if at all. Gentiles, people who had not been part of the Jewish community, began to hear and respond to the gospel. This presented a new problem. While Jesus had clearly associated with sinners and had made it clear that His message was for them, these had been Jewish sinners, now the gospel was reaching sinners who were not Jews at all but Gentiles.

A key transitional event in the spreading of the good news is the visit of Peter to the house of the God-fearing Gentile, Cornelius, recorded in Acts 10:1–11:18.

This is a remarkable story of God's intervention. At stake was the spread of the gospel beyond the Jewish world. For this to happen it was necessary to change Peter's wrong attitude towards 'sinners' and at the same time prepare the ground for the message of Jesus to go beyond the boundaries of Jewish thought.

Peter was a Jew, he had been circumcised and he valued the customs of the Jewish people. Now he was a follower of Jesus, who had come for sinners, and he was about to encounter a person who was not from a Jewish background.

Cornelius was a God-fearing Gentile who lived in Caesarea. Luke records that one day, at about three in the afternoon, Cornelius had a vision of an angel. The angel told him to send some men to the city of Joppa to bring back a man called Simon Peter. This was clearly not an everyday event, God's intervention is supernatural and specific, and it wasn't only Cornelius who had a vision.

About noon the day after this, Simon Peter who was just outside Joppa, ascended the roof of the house where he was staying, to pray. He fell into a trance and had a vision during which he was told to kill and eat ceremonially unclean meat. This vision is very significant, it helped Peter to begin to understand that he was not bound by Jewish custom and tradition – nothing is unclean that God makes clean!

Immediately after this revelation, while Peter was still thinking about it, Cornelius' messengers arrived and explained to him that Cornelius had sent them to bring him back to meet him. Peter and some of the brothers then set out with them to Caesarea.

When they arrived in Caesarea it became clear why God had intervened in such a special way. Peter's change of mind was to be vital, as he said to the people who had gathered: 'You are well aware that it is against our law for a Jew to associate with a Gentile or visit him. But God has shown me that I should not call any man impure or unclean. So when I was sent for, I came without raising any objection. May I ask why you sent for me?' (10:28–29).

Peter had learned that he should not see Gentiles as 'unclean', people to avoid and stay away from for fear of making himself unclean. He had leapt a chasm in this change of attitude. John Stott, in his commentary *Message of Acts*, comments:

It is difficult for us to grasp the impassable gulf which yawned in those days between Jews on the one hand and the Gentiles (including even the 'God-fearers') on the other. Not that the Old Testament itself countenanced such a divide. On the contrary, alongside its oracles against the hostile nations, it affirmed that God had a purpose for them. By choosing and blessing one family, he intended to bless all the families of the earth. So psalmists and prophets foretold the day when God's Messiah would inherit the nations, the Lord's servant would be their light, all the nations would 'flow' to the Lord's house, and God would pour out his Spirit on all humankind. *The tragedy was that Israel twisted the doctrine of election into one of favouritism*, became filled with racial pride and hatred, despised Gentiles as 'dogs' *and developed traditions which kept them apart*. No orthodox Jew would ever enter the home of a Gentile, even a God-fearer, or invite such into his home. On the contrary, 'all familiar intercourse with Gentiles was forbidden' and 'no pious Jew would of course have sat down at the table of a Gentile'. (my italics)[3]

The tragedy that Stott helpfully explains was that the Jews had come to see their status as God's people as something that distanced them from those outside. This was never God's intention. Peter as a Jew who now followed Jesus needed to have his mind changed and his natural objections supernaturally overcome.

Peter had been with Jesus, had heard the grumbling and moaning of the Pharisees when Jesus went to the homes of sinners. Peter had heard Jesus' hard words towards the Pharisees, and His message that God loves sinners. Now he has to work this out for himself, and here was a new dimension. Cornelius was a Gentile, he was not a sinful Jew but an outsider. Small wonder that Peter needed supernatural vision to help him!

The words that Peter spoke next are perhaps some of the most profound and important words recorded in the New Testament. They introduce a new era, the dawn of a new understanding of God's love and mercy. He said: 'I now realise how true it is that God does not show favouritism but accepts men from every nation who fear him and do what is right' (Acts 10:34–35). These verses are pivotal; if Peter had not realised this, the message would not have got beyond Judea. Now at last he had seen that the things Jesus said regarding self-righteousness were not only true of the Pharisees. He, like them, due to his customs, had seen God as only showing favour to people who were circumcised. Now he saw that God's mercy was not favouritism expressed to a certain group of people – it was for all.

It was this realisation that enabled him to communicate the message of Jesus to a Gentile and declare '… that everyone who believes in him receives forgiveness of sins through his name' (v.43). The key phrase here is 'everyone who believes'. God's mercy is not restricted, it is available to 'everyone'. And the message spoken in the house of Cornelius was accompanied by the same spiritual power as the message Peter had communicated in Jerusalem.

> While Peter was still speaking these words, the Holy Spirit came on all who heard the message. The circumcised believers who had come with Peter were astonished that the gift of the Holy Spirit had been poured out *even on* the Gentiles. For they heard them speaking in tongues and praising God. Then Peter said, 'Can anyone keep these people from being baptised with water? They have received the Holy Spirit just as we have.' So he ordered that they be baptised in the name of Jesus Christ. (10:44–48, my italics)

The circumcised believers who were with Peter were *astonished* that *even* the Gentiles could receive the Holy Spirit. This did not match their view that God only blessed His 'favoured' people. Something now was clearly happening. God the Holy Spirit was not restricted to those who had been circumcised, but was for all people. Now these early believers were beginning to experience for themselves the potency of the words of Jesus, He really had come to seek and to save *the lost*!

Peter's response is interesting: 'Can anyone keep these people from being baptised with water?' Circumcision, the Jewish covenant sign of being part of the people of God, began to be replaced as the 'way in' to God's kingdom. Baptism in water and by the Holy Spirit for the forgiveness of sins began to be the method of entry, because it signified that it is because of God's mercy; and who can keep these people from receiving God's mercy?

I can't help reflecting back to the incident of the woman caught in adultery (John 8) where the accusers wanted to stone her for her sin. 'Who among you has not sinned?' was Jesus' retort. This incident is a benchmark – there is no favouritism, all people regardless of their religious background can only know God because of His mercy and sacrifice – there is no distinction.

Jesus' commission was being fulfilled, the good news that God loves the lost was spreading beyond previous boundaries. The lost were being found and if the Early Church followed the pattern of Jesus' teaching in His parables then there would be a celebration. But it didn't happen, not immediately anyway. Their first response was to display their surprise that Peter had associated with Gentiles and had gone into the home of a Gentile. 'The apostles and the brothers throughout Judea heard that the Gentiles also had received the word of God. So when Peter went up to Jerusalem, the circumcised believers criticised him and said, 'You went into the house of uncircumcised men and ate with them' (Acts 11:1–3).

This natural reaction was overcome when Peter explained that what had happened was the fulfilment of what Jesus had promised:

'As I began to speak, the Holy Spirit came on them as he had come on us at the beginning. Then I remembered what the Lord had said: "John baptised with water, but you will be baptised with the Holy Spirit." So if God gave them the same gift as he gave us, who believed in the Lord Jesus Christ, who was I to think that I could oppose God?' (Acts 11:15–17)

Peter's explanation was enough for the believers in Jerusalem. Luke records, 'When they heard this, they had no further objections and praised God, saying, "So then, God has granted even the Gentiles repentance unto life"' (11:18). Their conclusion was the same as that of the circumcised believers who were with Peter in the house of Cornelius – even the Gentiles 'have been granted repentance unto life'.

So the door was opening, the good news of God's gift of mercy, regardless of religious tradition, was beginning to transform lives. This incident paved the way for the gospel to break out from its Jewish context and begin to transform the Gentile world.

Immediately after their realisation that the good news was for everyone, Luke records in the very next verse, 'Now those who had been scattered by the persecution associated with Stephen travelled as far as Phoenicia,

Cyprus and Antioch, telling the message only to Jews' (v.19).

This 'telling the message only to Jews' is what would have been expected; they did what had been done up until now, but then, Luke records, 'Some of them, however, men from Cyprus and Cyrene, went to Antioch and began to speak to Greeks also, telling them the good news about the Lord Jesus' (v.20).

The 'Gentiles' referred to in verse 18 are more specifically called 'Greeks' in verse 20. It is worth spending a few moments thinking about who these 'Greeks' in Antioch were.

Greeks in Antioch

Antioch was not in Greece but in Syria and had been built as part of the Greek empire. It was a very cosmopolitan city with Greeks, Jews, Romans, Persians, Indians and Chinese. This multi-racial urban metropolis sounds rather like most major cities in the world today. Despite their variety of backgrounds, many would have spoken the common language Greek. It was this that led to the definition 'Greeks' being attributed to those living in Antioch – a variety of people, but who spoke Greek.

A number of these 'Greeks' were in fact Jews. Unlike other ancient cities where the Jews were a despised group, here the Jewish population was large, many were Jewish converts, their status was high and they enjoyed the rights of full citizens. Perhaps most importantly, the barriers between Jew and Gentile were very slight.

So, in Antioch, the good news was told to an audience that was not exclusively 'Jewish'. This is therefore a step on from Jerusalem. However, many of the 'Greeks' of Antioch would have had some exposure to and understanding of 'the God of Israel'. This mix of Jewish influence alongside a whole host of other world-views and beliefs provided the Christians with a tremendous opportunity and challenge.

This diverse group heard, as Luke records, 'The good news about the Lord Jesus' (v.20).

Luke doesn't tell us how they went about telling the good news. A hint though is to be found in his omission of the title 'Christ', which is the Greek word for Messiah. The Jews were waiting for the Messiah to come and therefore would have been familiar with the word and all that it conveyed. The 'Greeks' however were not familiar with the term and therefore when the gospel was communicated for the first time to these non-Jewish Greeks it appears that 'Christ' was not used and therefore at first Jesus was not presented as the Christ* (Messiah), or as the fulfilment of God's promises in Scripture as had been the case in Peter's 'Pentecost sermon' in Jerusalem.

In Antioch Jesus was referred to as 'the Lord', a title just as true and which would connect with people who believed in 'gods' and 'lords'. By introducing Jesus as 'the Lord' these Christians proclaimed the 'good news' in such a way that the audience would see its relevance and importance to them. The title 'Lord' established common ground in a way that 'Messiah' would not. This different approach is important to note. The Church could not assume that people would understand the message – unless it was communicated in a way that made sense to those who were hearing it.

It was into this diverse but tolerant atmosphere that the gospel was communicated in a way that did not depart from the message of Jesus, but translated it into a form of words that would make sense to the hearers. It certainly seemed to hit the mark. Luke records: 'The Lord's hand was with them, and a great number of people believed and turned to the Lord' (11:21). The door was opening even wider, more lost people were being found; heaven must have been really celebrating and so too surely the Church. But once again it didn't happen, not immediately anyway.

Things, it seems, are never simple. The struggle to keep the message of Jesus pure became more heightened as a result of the gospel transforming the lives of people with little or no Jewish background.

Many who had come to faith in Jesus from a Jewish background were not happy that those from a non-Jewish background could be welcomed into the community of believers without observing the correct customs and traditions. And this explosion wasn't restricted to Antioch. F.F. Bruce describes what happened:

---

*This does not mean that the title 'Christ' was never used. Only that it was not the most appropriate title by which to attract the minds of this new audience. It must have been used eventually because the disciples were first called Christians – something of a nickname – at Antioch.

But the trouble was not confined to Antioch. Not long after, it broke out in the recently formed churches of the province of Galatia, in Pisidian Antioch, Iconium, Lystra and Derbe. These churches received visits from some Judaizing Christians who urged upon them (as something over and above what Barnabas and Paul had taught them) the necessity of adding to their faith in Christ circumcision and observance of the Jewish ceremonial law.[4]

These Judaising Christians were those that had come to faith in Jesus from a Jewish background and insisted that in addition to faith in Jesus, new believers should follow the customs of Judaism and be circumcised.

Something was stirring, the wind of the Spirit was 'blowing where he wills' and the leaders of the Early Church had to grapple with how to maintain an effective witness of these new communities that were increasingly being formed among people who did not have a Jewish background.

Luke records a great deal concerning the situation in Antioch and it is important to look at this in some depth as the problem wasn't a local one. What was experienced at Antioch was happening all over.

The church in Antioch – transform or conform?

Soon after the initial response to the good news, Barnabas, and then Paul with him, spent a year in Antioch. Luke records, 'So for a whole year Barnabas and Saul met with the church and taught great numbers of people' (Acts 11:26). This new church began to grow and develop as lives were transformed by the Holy Spirit. Then a little later Luke records these key verses:

> Some men came down from Judea to Antioch and were teaching the brothers: 'Unless you are circumcised, according to the custom taught by Moses, you cannot be saved.' This brought Paul and Barnabas into sharp dispute and debate with them. So Paul and Barnabas were appointed, along with some other believers, to go up to Jerusalem to see the apostles and elders about this question.' (15:1–2)

This dispute had to be worked out because at stake was the very message of Jesus. Jesus had said that His message was for the lost, and that it was God's mercy, not the observance of religious customs, that would save them. Now the lost were responding, but many of those from a Jewish background found it impossible to separate the message of Jesus from their customs and traditions. For the sake of the non-Jewish a solution had to be found. Once again the preservation of the pure message of Jesus was at a critical stage. If the transforming message of God's mercy had been concealed behind the need to conform to Jewish customs, then the power of the message to transform the lives of those who were not familiar with Judaism would have been lost.

This 'dispute' became the context for a great debate that took place in AD 59, at the 'Council of Jerusalem'. During the debate, some believers who belonged to the part of the Pharisees said, 'The Gentiles must be circumcised and required to obey the law of Moses' (15:5). After further discussion, Peter addressed the apostles and elders:

> 'Brothers, you know that some time ago God made a choice among you that the Gentiles might hear from my lips the message of the gospel and believe. God, who knows the heart, showed that he accepted them by giving the Holy Spirit to them, just as he did to us. He made *no distinction* between us and them, for he purified their hearts by faith. Now then, why do you try to test God by putting on the necks of the disciples a yoke that neither we nor our fathers have been able to bear? No! We believe it is through the grace of our Lord Jesus that we are saved, just as they are.' (Acts 15:7–11, my italics)

It is worth noting some key points made by Peter in this address.

1. God shows no distinction – salvation is the result of God's initiative, not man's religious efforts. Therefore being a Jew or a Gentile does not carry any merit as far as salvation is concerned.
2. Salvation involves the heart being purified by faith. This again is God's initiative and its result is transformation in the life of the believer.
3. Consequently, observing or conforming to customs and habits that

cannot bring about this purified heart should not be imposed upon those whom God has accepted. This cannot be right because even the Jews could not earn salvation by observing these!

Grace

As a defining summary of these points, Peter introduced a word to describe what Jesus achieved through His life, death and resurrection. His closing sentence introduced the phrase 'through the grace of our Lord Jesus'. The word 'grace' became increasingly used to describe what faith in Jesus meant. We will look at this in more detail when we consider how Paul handled this issue.

Following Peter's speech, and the testimony from Paul and Barnabas regarding all the signs and wonders that God was doing among the Gentiles, James concluded that God had plainly chosen Gentiles as well as Jews. He supported his conclusion by referring to the Scriptures, which clearly show that the Gentiles are included in God's salvation plan. He then stated, 'It is my judgment, therefore, that we should not make it difficult for the Gentiles who are turning to God' (Acts 15:19).

The result of the Council of Jerusalem was that, 'It was decided that no other condition than faith in Christ should be imposed on the Gentiles, as necessary either for salvation or for fellowship with their Jewish fellow-believers.'[5] A key matter still had to be considered – the practical outworking of this decision. How would those who had always had to live by these customs get along with those who were not required to? The decision of the Council was to write a letter explaining what it would like the Gentile believers to do that they might live alongside and in fellowship with the Jewish believers.

The letter instructed them not only to abstain from idolatry, which they had already done in view of their commitment to Christ, but also everything that had idolatrous associations, such as food that had been sacrificed to pagan deities. They were also instructed to conform to the Jewish practice of not eating blood and to bring their sexual code into line with the Jewish marriage laws, which were based on the Old Testament.

Again there are some key points that are worth noting.

1. Those who already have received salvation do not have everything right. Believers should never be arrogant and impose their customs onto new believers.
2. Churches should not scrap everything they do in favour of those coming in because some of what they do is valuable, and both the existing and the new people have to be able to get along together.
3. The key factor seems to be – what will aid the process of the gospel? Faith expressing itself through love should, it seems, be the driving force behind how the Church functions and organises itself.

But one meeting, as is so often the case, did not solve everything. Many of the churches that were planted at the beginning had to face the same question. As the Holy Spirit awakened people in cities across the world to faith in Jesus, so the Judaisers sought to impose Jewish customs upon them. Indeed much of the rest of the New Testament following on from Acts is made up of letters written to the new churches. The dominant theme in these letters is that it is 'grace' not 'law' that results in salvation. And it is this theme of grace not law that provides the backdrop for most of the letters written to the early churches by the apostle Paul.

Paul

Paul wrote his letters to specific communities of believers, addressing specific situations. These letters, written during a period when these first communities were still forming, deal primarily with the same question that Jesus had addressed in His message, and the apostles had then preached as they travelled. Now that these communities were forming, it became vital to ensure that Jesus' message was not corrupted.

Again, as with Jesus' teaching in Luke, it is important to understand the context of Paul's teaching in order to really grasp its significance. There were two key words that he used as he sought to convince the early believers to stay true to the message of Jesus.

Firstly, 'grace', the word that Peter had used at the Jerusalem Council. Then the second key word for Paul was 'justification'. In using these terms Paul wanted to demonstrate that salvation was not the result of observance of the law and custom. There was no merit on the part of man – salvation was in no sense earned, nor was it a reward. Salvation for Paul was the free gift of God and was achieved as a result of the cross and resurrection of Jesus. It is all of grace – the language of grace vibrates with passionate gratitude throughout his letters.

Of the many places that could be looked at where Paul talks about grace, I have chosen to start in Galatians, because here he explicitly provides the context for his appeal to believers not to depart from the message of Jesus. He introduces the theme by referring to an incident involving a dispute between himself and the apostle Peter.

When Peter came to Antioch, I opposed him to his face, because he was clearly in the wrong. Before certain men came from James, he used to eat with the Gentiles. But when they arrived, he began to draw back and separate himself from the Gentiles because he was afraid of those who belonged to the circumcision group. The other Jews joined him in his hypocrisy, so that by their hypocrisy even Barnabas was led astray.

When I saw that they were not acting in line with the truth of the gospel, I said to Peter in front of them all, 'You are a Jew, yet you live like a Gentile and not like a Jew. How is it, then, that you force Gentiles to follow Jewish customs?

'We who are Jews by birth and not "Gentile sinners" know that a man is not justified by observing the law, but by faith in Jesus Christ. So we, too, have put our faith in Christ Jesus that we may be justified by faith in Christ and not by observing the law, because by observing the law no-one will be justified.' (Gal. 2:11–16)

Paul applies this dispute to the Galatians' situation, telling them that neither should they be talked into doing these things. He speaks directly to them, saying, 'I am astonished that you are so quickly deserting the one who called you by the grace of Christ and are turning to a different gospel – which is really no gospel at all' (1:6).

Paul then continued to explain this 'different gospel':

You foolish Galatians! Who has bewitched you? Before your very eyes Jesus Christ was clearly portrayed as crucified. I would like to learn just one thing from you: Did you receive the Spirit by observing the law, or by believing what you heard? Are you so foolish? After beginning with the Spirit, are you now trying to attain your goal by human effort? (3:1–3)

He then underlined:

You are all sons of God through faith in Christ Jesus, for all of you who were baptised into Christ have clothed yourselves with Christ. There is neither Jew nor Greek, slave nor free, male nor female, for you are all one in Christ Jesus. (3:26–28)

He reached a crescendo:

For in Christ Jesus neither circumcision nor uncircumcision has any value. The only thing that counts is faith expressing itself through love. (5:6)

Paul's passion and urgency is obvious in this letter, he is desperate to preserve the message of Jesus, he does not want it to be concealed behind the unnecessary observance of customs and law that cannot save. It is grace, God's gift of mercy, not man's effort, that results in salvation. This salvation is only possible because of Jesus!

This theme is developed in Paul's letter to the Romans.

But now a righteousness from God, apart from law, has been made known, to which the Law and the Prophets testify. This righteousness from God comes through faith in Jesus Christ to all who believe. There is no difference, for all have sinned and fall short of the glory of God, and are justified freely by his grace through the redemption that came by Christ Jesus. (Rom. 3:21–24)

This section contains a favourite verse that is used to communicate the Christian message today. The sentence 'All have sinned and fall short of the glory of God' (Rom. 3:23), often appears on tracts and is used to demonstrate to unchurched people living today that they are sinners. I am not denying the truth of that but clearly this was not the context of the verse. Romans 3:23 starts with the word 'for' suggesting that what is about to be said is related to what has just been said. The preceding verses state: 'But now a righteousness from God, apart from the law, has been made known, to which the Law and the Prophets testify. This righteousness from God comes through faith in Jesus Christ to all who believe. There is no difference' (3:21–22).

Paul said this, not to condemn the sinner but to underline the message Jesus gave the religious leaders, that Peter contended for after his meeting with Cornelius, and that Paul, Barnabas and Peter stood for at the Jerusalem Council. Paul was saying that the law cannot save, it is only Jesus! As Peter had said in Antioch, 'It is through the grace of our Lord Jesus that we are saved, just as they are.' This is because 'God made no distinction between us and them' (Acts 15:9). Now to the Romans Paul says, 'There is no difference.' It is not those who trust in their observance of the law who are saved, it is those who trust in Jesus for mercy. At no point can the believer say that faith is as a result of personal merit, this would be to misunderstand the message of Jesus and the grace of God.

Paul underlined this further in Romans 3:24, saying that all are 'justified freely by his grace'. And then again, in verse 27, he recalls the same theme that Jesus had addressed in the house of the Pharisee in Acts 14. 'Where, then, is boasting? It is excluded. On what principle? On that of observing the law? No, but on that of faith.'

Charles Hodge, in his commentary on Romans, puts it like this: 'This righteousness, of which God is the author, and which is available before him, and which is now revealed, is more particularly described as a righteousness which is of faith, i.e. by means *of* faith, not *on account* of faith. Faith is not the ground of our justification; it is not the righteousness which makes us righteous before God.' [6]

We have to be so careful even when using the phrase 'justified by faith', because we can so easily turn faith into 'that which saves us'. Believing the right doctrines, and following the right customs, can become the new way of self-justification.

William Hendriksen, in his commentary, adds: 'This light, this ray of optimism, comes not from below but from above. It is "a righteousness from God." It is he who comes to the rescue. It is he who condescends to save those who had made themselves thoroughly unworthy of being saved.'[7]

Grace, for Paul, must not be conceived in any way as the divine mercy coming to the aid of man in his own efforts to be righteous. Grace is not God coming to our aid, because this still carries the idea that salvation is earned with a little help from God along the way. This is how those who were from a Jewish background would have understood it. But Paul underlined again and again that grace was not God helping us, it is a whole new life on a whole new basis, set free from sin and Satan, empowered with the Holy Spirit. Grace is not merely, therefore, one helpful aspect of the Christian life; it is the presupposition of the whole Christian life – everything stems from this grace. It is not surprising, therefore, that each of Paul's letters begins with a grace greeting and ends with a grace farewell.

Here, and in many other places, Paul passionately opposed any tampering with the good news of grace. He was utterly and totally committed to ensuring that Jesus' message was not changed and used as a basis for any form of self-righteousness. He knew how damaging it would be for the mission of the Church if the message were robbed of its grace and turned into a list of rules that nobody can keep and that could never save!

Paul could see, and clearly addressed, the problem that could have prevented the spread of the message of Jesus. The good news of mercy had to be preserved!

Summary

And so, at the end of the era of Jesus and the apostles, the Church was still emerging and developing. It had not yet become an institution, but through many trials and conflicts the message of Jesus had been retained … and then!

After the apostles – the message is concealed

Then things changed.

But not straightaway. Through the ministry of the apostles and many others the Christian message spread across the world, accompanied by the Person and power of the Holy Spirit. As the first 100 to 200 years passed, lives and communities were transformed, as people from many backgrounds became followers of Jesus.

It is difficult to be precise about all that went on during this period. It seems clear, however, that as the message of Jesus spread across the world and new communities were formed, some themes began to emerge. These would have huge implications regarding the message that was preached in the years that followed. They were largely a response to the circumstances in which the message was being communicated. We'll take a look at the background in those early years.

Challenges from outside the Church

Persecution and martyrdom

In some parts of the world today, Christians are still being persecuted, even losing their lives, for their faith in Jesus. For many of us, the most we have to fear is that those we are trying to reach will just ignore us or perhaps think we are a little strange.

However, the birth and infancy of the Church was in the context of violent opposition. It is for this reason that the Greek word for witness, 'martyr', began to mean something more specific than just telling others about Jesus, but became associated with those who literally died for the faith. The witness of many early Christians was to result in their death. Stories of remarkable heroism and accounts of God's presence in the midst of these trials are awe-inspiring. These early witnesses/martyrs stood against all that was thrown at them by rulers and emperors who wanted to wipe out this new sect that encouraged people to worship Jesus. Consequently, martyrdom began to be seen, quite understandably, as a noble and meritorious act.

The 'martyrs' were a huge inspiration to the Early Church, but many followers of Jesus were not so courageous and considered giving up on their faith. They needed encouragement and support just to carry on. It's not surprising really, stories of heroism are inspiring to us and would have been to them, but I don't think many of us reading this can imagine what it is like to live literally in fear of our lives because of our faith in Jesus.

Emergence of strong leaders

It is no surprise either that during this period of persecution strong leadership grew up; leaders who often did not have the luxury of developing the gifts and skills of all those in the Body, but who championed the cause of the faith and upon whom many believers came to depend. The early presbyters/elders and bishops carried great responsibility and increasingly great authority as the Church went through these early trials. While the titles elders and bishops are still used today, their role is very different to those of the leaders in the Early Church.

As a result of bravery, heroism, God's presence and strong leadership, and against all the odds humanly speaking, the Church not only survived severe persecution but emerged as a strong and international movement.

As well as the challenges from those who tried to extinguish the Christian faith there were challenges within.

Challenges from within the Church

As the movement reached many different parts of the world, it began to face a challenge that would become an increasingly important issue over the next couple of centuries. The challenge was how to define the Christian faith in a way that was consistent.

No common 'rule of faith'

Communities were being formed in many different parts of the world and being joined by people from a variety of backgrounds. Some of what they had believed they brought with them, and were now coming to terms with just exactly what faith in Jesus really meant. Churches in one part of the world saw things differently from those in another and it became important to begin to define a rule of faith that described who Jesus was and what it meant to follow Him, to define what Christians really believed. There was, at this time, no New Testament; some churches had received letters from apostles, which may have been circulated to other churches, and the Gospels were also in circulation, but there was no actual 'rule of faith' as we have it today in the Bible.

As the Church made huge advances across the world, and as communities were formed, things began to be put into place that would enable the Church to continue to grow and develop in a hostile world. It is difficult to be absolutely sure of all that was happening during this period as the Church became more identified as a world-wide movement. Here is not the place to analyse this in great depth, but what is important for the purposes of this book, is that there is a clear relationship between the developments that took place and the message that was communicated.

The Apostolic Fathers

In addition to the writings of the apostles which were later collected and included in what we call the New Testament, there were other key leaders within the emerging Church who wrote soon after the period covered in the Acts of the Apostles. These leaders are often referred to as the Apostolic Fathers. Their writings provide fascinating insights into how the original message of Jesus and the apostles was slowly reinterpreted. The result of this process was that eventually the message of grace, regardless of observance of ritual and custom, was replaced by a message where once again entry into the kingdom of God was perceived as being earned by observance of a new set of rituals and customs. Christian customs replaced Jewish customs but, at the heart, the message of grace was lost.

While many of the Fathers could be referred to, I have concentrated briefly on just a few. These highlight most simply what began to happen to the message of Jesus and the apostles as it became the responsibility of the leaders within the Church after the apostles.

Ignatius

The dramatic and courageous story of Ignatius, born in AD 50 who became the bishop of Antioch, is a telling example of how what is done and said for all the right reasons can result in departure from the truth.

Ignatius was a leader within the Church during the time of persecution and he died a martyr's death following sentence by the Roman Emperor Trajan. At his sentencing, Trajan pronounced: 'We command that Ignatius, who affirms that he carries about within Him that was crucified, be bound by soldiers, and carried to the great (city) Rome, there to be devoured by the beasts, for the gratification of the people.'

On hearing his sentence, Ignatius cried out with joy, 'I thank Thee, O Lord, that Thou hast vouchsafed to honour me with a perfect love towards Thee, and hast made me to be bound with iron chains, like Thy Apostle Paul.'

He writes in chapter 4 of his letter to the Romans: 'I am God's wheat, ground fine by the lion's teeth to be made pure bread for Christ.'

And then in chapter 6:

No earthly pleasures, no kingdoms of this world can benefit me in any way. I prefer death in Christ Jesus to power over the farthest limits of the earth. He who died in place of us is the one object of my quest. He who rose for our sakes is my one desire. The time for my birth is close at hand. Forgive me, my brothers. Do not stand in the way of my birth to real life; do not wish me stillborn. My desire is to belong to God. Do not, then, hand me back to the world. Do not try to tempt me with material things. Let me attain pure light. Only on my arrival there can I be fully a human being. Give me the privilege of imitating the passion of my God.

There is no question that the idea of dying a martyr's death was considered a great honour by Ignatius. And, while he was a true hero of the faith and one it is impossible not to admire, his emphasis on the honour of the martyr's death and subsequent glory, though admirable and heroic, subtly undermined the message of Jesus and the apostles. So without in any way seeking to diminish the courage and example of Ignatius, it is important to see how his teaching undermined their message.

Paul had said that faith 'justifies us'. It is only Jesus, and nothing that we ourselves can do. Ignatius, when writing to the Christians in Rome regarding his impending martyrdom, said: 'For in bonds in Christ Jesus I hope to salute you, if it be God's will that I should be accounted worthy to reach the end. For the beginning is well ordained if I may attain the end and so receive my inheritance without hindrance ... But for me it is difficult to attain unto God, unless you spare me.'

These impassioned words are perfectly understandable in the light of what was to happen to Ignatius, but they say something very different to the teaching of Jesus and of Paul. Grace which is all of mercy, grace that results in the sinner being fully justified, is not present in these words. For Ignatius, this salvation was something that would be attained in the future, by virtue of his martyrdom. It was not observance of the law and customs for him that was meritorious, it was the act of martyrdom. He had unconsciously introduced a new form of merit that earned salvation.

However, it was not only in his letter to the Romans dealing with the matter of his martyrdom that Ignatius subtly undermined the apostolic message. Throughout his other epistles themes are present that use the language of the apostles, but begin to present the message in a different way. Paul had written in Galatians: 'The only thing that counts is faith expressing itself through love' (Gal. 5:6).

Ignatius used the words faith and love, but subtly began to express faith as that which earns salvation. This is because, for him, love was that which perfected faith. Love was the moral quality of doing the right thing and faith became faithfully living this way. As such, faithfully living the loving life resulted in the reward of being justified.

Ignatius introduced the *reward* of grace. Paul spoke of grace as stemming from God. Because of God's grace we have faith and because of that faith we live lives of love; it is in that order. Grace, for Paul, was the foundation upon which everything else was built. To put it simply:

$$\text{Grace} \longrightarrow \text{faith} + \text{love}.$$

Because of His love God has mercifully given us the gift of faith which results in our living loving lives, and an inheritance in His eternal kingdom.

But for Ignatius the equation was altogether different.

$$\text{Faith} + \text{love} \longrightarrow \text{Grace}.$$

In other words, because we live faithful loving lives God will allow us to attain entry into His eternal kingdom and grace is now the reward for faith not the cause of it! The means has become the end!

Thus, subtly, even though the same words have been used, the message of Jesus and the apostles has been undermined. Once again God's love is something that is perceived as being earned as a result of what we do rather than a free gift resulting from what God has done in Christ.

Then Ignatius took things one step further. In other of his writings he concentrated a great deal on church unity. This unity found its basis in the fact that Christ is one with the Father. Ignatius applied a similar unity to the leaders of the Church, the bishops. He expressed that, however distant they may be from one another in different parts of the world, they are all at one with Jesus Christ.

This high view of the status of the bishops led to an insistence that members of the congregation should not resist them. Thus it was by gathering in the congregation and not resisting the bishop that lives could be lived properly in submission to God. It is by being part of the congregation, being members of this organism, that a person can participate in the life of God. Here are the beginnings of what would become an increasingly dominant theme. That salvation takes place and is somehow earned by virtue of being present in the congregation.

Other writings

Other writings of the Fathers reveal this tendency towards justification by attainment as opposed to grace. As with Ignatius, these writings did not set out to undermine the message of Jesus. They sought to make sense of it in a world that was lawless and chaotic and in which the message of Jesus was impacting such diverse groups of people.

The Epistle of Barnabas was written against a backdrop of large-scale lawlessness and impending catastrophe. In such a world, the author felt, it was presumptuous for Christians to think of themselves as justified already. Justification, he felt, belonged to the future. Believers cannot be sure that they are justified, they can only hope to be saved and to attain life. The epistle includes these words: 'By thy hands thou shalt work for the redemption of thy sins.'

Once again grace was presented as the reward for, not the cause of, living the Christian life.

Add to this the comment of *Clement of Rome* in his second epistle. He writes: 'Fasting is better than prayer but the giving of alms is better than both' (J.B. Lightfoot translation). Of course almsgiving is a good thing. The giving of money to help the poor or to support others in the Christian community who have lost their homes and possessions due to their faith in Christ, must be good. The danger comes when the giving of alms begins to be seen as a meritorious act, something that earns salvation. This development can be seen in the writing of Cyprian.

Writing in the third century on the subject of almsgiving, he says: 'As water quenches fire, so do alms quench sin.'

It is not possible to know how widespread or universally believed the writings of the Fathers were but these few excerpts do expose a trend that was beginning to take hold in the emerging Church. Jesus had taught that salvation was not earned by merit and the apostles had fought vigorously to preserve this message. But slowly, the writings and influence of the Apostolic Fathers, as they sought to lead the Church through persecution, and into becoming a universal community, led to a reinterpretation of Jesus' message. Their understanding of the message greatly influenced the way that the Church structured itself as it emerged from being a persecuted movement to eventually becoming the religion of Rome. Much of what was to happen as the Church defined its faith and practice, owed more to the influence of the Fathers than to Jesus and the apostles.

Defining the faith

While the Church was still developing, it had other issues to resolve which were fundamental to its survival. Christianity was a faith, a faith that was unfortunately increasingly perceived as a reward for good works. Nevertheless this faith needed to be defined. By the second century the Church had grown in a dramatic way across the world. This 'Church' was not a large number of independent communities, rather it was understood as being the 'Church Catholic'. (The term 'Catholic' – universal – demonstrated that the Church was one ecumenical body throughout the world. It did not, at this stage, refer to a particular denomination but was a 'description' of what the Church was.) This Church consisted of a number of 'local and visible' communities, but these communities formed one 'Body'. And this one Body needed to be united around one truth. Hence the beginnings of an agreed canon of truth can be seen by the dawning of the third century. As F.F. Bruce writes:

> ... as many things were being taught thus in various quarters which were warmly disputed in others, we find the Church Catholic defining with increasing precision the beliefs which it regarded as true. At the end of the second century, then, we can recognise quite clearly the Catholic Church, the Catholic Canon, and the Catholic Faith.[1]

This 'defining with increasing precision the beliefs which it regarded as true' led to:

Conformity of belief

As time passed and the gospel reached more and more people, there was a gradual development of a 'canon of truth' that defined the content of the Christian faith. Increasingly, those people that wanted to join the Christian community were required to publicly confess that they had put their faith in Jesus. This was necessary as it was important that those who called themselves Christians understood what a Christian was, and were prepared to make a public declaration.

Baptismal confession

Entry into the Christian community followed baptism of the new believer and it was at the time of baptism that these confessions were made. It is interesting to observe what confession was required of those coming into the faith.

When new believers were formally admitted to the early Christian community by baptism, it was considered necessary that they should make a public confession of their new faith. This was probably in response to a definite question. Following their confession of Jesus as Lord, the new believers were baptised 'Into the name of the Lord Jesus' and from then onwards they were publicly known as members of the Christian community.[2]

This was actually more complicated than it sounds, because some of those trusting in Jesus had been Jews or 'God-fearing Gentiles', while others were from a non-Jewish background. For those who had become Christians but who were Jews by birth or else Gentiles who had already accepted much of the Jewish belief in one God, a simple baptismal confession was required. They had come to accept Jesus as the Messiah and Lord based on Old Testament revelation, and a simple confession of Jesus as 'Lord' or

'Son of God' at their baptism was enough to admit them into the Christian community.

The situation was altogether different as the gospel went to complete pagans. They had to learn about Jesus as Saviour and Lord, but also understand that God is One and that He is the Creator and righteous Judge. There was so much they did not know and therefore they were required to give a more detailed confession of faith than believing Jews or God-fearers. Their confession would be more than 'Jesus is Lord'. It would probably have been in answer to a question such as this:

> Do you believe in God the Father?
> And in Jesus Christ, His only Son, our Lord?
> And in the Holy Spirit?

The development of this baptismal confession demonstrates how the Early Church began to put together a framework of belief to which all who were to join the Christian community would agree. The baptismal confessions provided the framework for the later creeds of the Catholic Church. At this stage the Church was not developing exclusive doctrines but giving definition to what it had experienced. Later, as the content of the baptismal confessions was challenged by various heresies, the Church began to define its beliefs in more formal credal statements.

Thus entry into the community of believers began to be open only to those who confessed that they believed a number of things to be true. In Acts Luke describes, in uncomplicated terms, how 'the Lord added to their number daily those who were being saved'. Little is said about what they had to believe in order to be added, only that their hearts were changed! Now, as the Church increasingly encountered many different people from different backgrounds and with a variety of beliefs that were displaced as a result of their faith in Jesus, this faith had to be defined.

Creeds

The need to define the Christian faith became increasingly urgent as the third century passed into the fourth. Many from within the Church began to raise questions that seriously challenged the accepted truths of the Christian communities. These 'truths' could not be taken for granted, they had to be defended and defined.

> … when these early Christian thinkers undertook to find words which might give adequate expression to their belief about God, they were not philosophising idly, or deliberately trying to make the Christian faith difficult; they were endeavouring to do justice to the data of revelation and experience.[3]

It is tempting to think that all these people did was to make something simple complicated and that they should have just left things alone. But they couldn't, the questions raised were too serious to ignore. The non-Jewish world into which the Church was spreading did not immediately share the same assumptions as the followers of Judaism who had come to faith in Jesus. They had different views regarding the nature of God, the universe and, as a result, Jesus!

The Gnostics (from the Greek word *gnosis* – knowledge) were influencing Christian thought in the very early days. Some of the New Testament writings, and certainly those of Ignatius and Clement, address the heretical teaching of the Gnostics regarding the Person and nature of Jesus. Also, in the early days of the Church the Docetists began to teach that Jesus could not have been truly a man because matter is evil. Jesus therefore only appeared to be a man. Later, in the second century, the Marcionists denied that Jesus was the Son of the covenant God of the Old Testament.

It was not possible to ignore these movements merely because what they taught struck at the heart of the developing Christian faith.

> But the chief importance of Marcionism in the second century lies in the reaction which it provoked in the leaders of the apostolic churches.

Just as Marcion's canon stimulated the more precise defining of the New Testament by the Catholic Church, not to supersede but to supplement the canon of the Old Testament; so, more generally, Marcion's teaching led the Catholic Church to define its faith more carefully, in terms calculated to exclude a Marcionite interpretation. [4]

The need to finally 'define' the Christian faith arose early in the fourth century when Arias, a parish priest in Alexandria, challenged the bishop. Arias could not see how Jesus was fully God and a member of the Trinity. Jesus, for Arias, was a man in whom the divine Spirit lived. The movement 'Arianism' that grew up posed such a threat that the Church had finally to define its message.

This happened at the Council of Nicea in Asia Minor on 20 May, AD 325. Baptismal confessions and creeds were used by this Council to create what was to become the doctrine of the Catholic Church.

F.F. Bruce, referring to the Council of Nicea, comments: 'Unlike previous credal statements, the Creed of Nicea was not a baptismal confession but an expression of ecclesiastical doctrine.'[5]

Thus the Council of Nicea signalled the beginning of a new era in the spread of the Christian message. It was now defined, and to be called a Christian required that a person publicly accepted certain doctrines as being true. It was this acceptance that allowed that person to join the Christian community.

This was inevitable, the Christian faith had to have some definition but, alongside the increasing 'conformity of belief', was an accelerating conformity of practice. It wasn't just what Christians believed that was defined, it was what they did as well!

Conformity of practice

The Christian faith, like any other movement or organisation, had to put into place certain structures that would be identified as being associated with that faith. Hence the increasing uniformity of doctrine, not surprisingly, led to an even greater uniformity in the things that Christians did. What had once been 'meeting together' became services or acts of worship. And these acts of worship took place in buildings that were immediately recognisable as Christian. Informal meetings in public places which had been a feature of the first believers, were replaced. Christians met in 'Christian' buildings and followed a Christian ritual. These rituals were increasingly led by clergy (from the Greek *Klerikos*, meaning inheritance); and the laity (from the Greek *laos*, meaning people) took part by observing the rituals.

The following excerpt from *Early Church History* by Backhouse and Tylor is long but it gives some idea as to just how things had changed since the time of the apostles.

… Enough has already been said to show that in the period 200 to 337 there was no check on the growth of ritualistic observances, but the substitution of external forms in place of primitive simplicity was still going on, and with constantly increasing force.

The worship of the apostolic age was without altars, without temples, without images, but as sacerdotal ideas entered and prevailed, ancient simplicity disappeared. The common meal, in which the early Christians united to commemorate their saviour's love, became a sacrifice; the table at which they sat to partake of it became an altar; the community which Christ designed to be one body was divided into clergy and laity. When the liberty of prophesying was lost, and the spiritual gifts promised to the congregation were exercised by a restricted order of ministers alone, those ministers became priests; whilst the simple effusions of Gospel love prompted by the Holy Spirit, and therefore powerful to break in pieces the stony and bind up the broken heart, were replaced by learned and eloquent discourses, which were even at times received with plaudits, as in a theatre. Lastly, the room or simple meeting-house was exchanged for a stately temple, richly furnished with gold and silver vessels. Even the wise Dionysius of Alexandria so completely loses sight of the New Covenant idea, as to call the table at which the bread and wine were partaken of, the 'Holy of Holies'.[6]

Such was the structure of Church that, probably in the fourth century, the Apostolical Constitutions contained the following description of an act of worship:

Let the building be long, with the head towards the east, and the vestries at the end on each side. Let the bishop's throne be set in the middle, with the seats for the presbytery on either hand, the deacons standing near in close-girt garments. Let the laity sit on the opposite side, with all quietness and good order; the women by themselves, also keeping silence. Let the reader stand on a raised place and read from the [Old Testament], and when two lessons have been read, let another sing hymns of David, and let the people join at the conclusion of the verses. Afterwards let there be a reading from the [New Testament], the presbyters and deacons and all the people standing with profound silence, for it is written, 'Be silent, and hear, O Israel.' Then let the presbyters one by one exhort the people, and lastly the bishop, as being chief over all. Let the porters stand at the doors where the men enter, and take notice of them, and the deaconesses at those of the women; and if any one be found sitting out of place, let the deacon rebuke him. Let the young people sit by themselves, if there be a place for them; if not let them stand, the younger women behind the older. Let the parents take charge of little children; the married women their children by themselves. Let the deacon watch over the congregation, that no one whisper or slumber, or laugh or nod.[7]

It is staggering to see how things have changed; even allowing for the fact that perhaps the first churches were not always completely spontaneous and as Spirit-led as we sometimes imagine. Nevertheless the Church here is now unrecognisable from what it had been in its earliest days. Also the leadership had changed. The same words were used to describe the leaders but their roles and functions were drastically different.

Conformity triumphs as the means of entry into the Christian community

The process of increasing conformity of belief and conformity of practice took a dramatic step forward following the remarkable experiences of the Roman emperor Constantine who, following a victorious battle at the Milvian Bridge in 312, became the Master of the Western Empire.

It was during his reign that many of the strands that had been developing over the previous couple of centuries began to be woven together. The result was a whole new era for the Church and the communication of a message that was far from the message of Jesus and the apostles.

M.A Smith comments:

> When Constantine marched into Rome after winning the Battle of the Milvian Bridge (312), he probably felt as if he had just touched something very powerful which he did not fully comprehend. He had gone into action against Maxentius, trusting in the sign of the Christians' God; and rather unexpectedly he was entering Rome as a victor.
>
> Here was a new and powerful God, who had favoured him. And at all costs Constantine must keep on the right side of Him. Anything which would upset the proper worship of this ultra-powerful deity could not be tolerated. Such a God would make too powerful an enemy, were Constantine to risk His displeasure. And so, throughout the rest of his reign, one of Constantine's main aims was to see that the Empire and the imperial dynasty continued to receive God's blessing.[8]

Up until the time of Constantine Christianity had been, in varying degrees, a persecuted faith; that was all to change.

This battle gave Constantine control of the Western Empire and later in his reign he conquered the Eastern Empire and eventually all persecution of Christians ceased as he announced a policy of religious tolerance throughout the whole empire. Christianity, though, was not merely 'tolerated', it became fashionable. As Henry Chadwick writes, 'The conversion of Constantine marks a turning-point in the history of the church and of Europe.'[9]

Constantine and a new 'acceptable' Christianity

This 'turning point' that took place during the reign of Constantine heralds the triumph of conformity as the means to entering the Christian community. A new challenge facing the Church was that their 'audience' became increasingly 'christianised' people. For early Christians the call to follow Jesus was often costly – even at the expense of their lives. The 'Jewish sect' that had spread throughout the world and had suffered persecution and opposition now, for the first time, was 'acceptable'. Under Constantine, rather than being persecuted for being a Christian it began to be advantageous.

Fashionable Christianity

Constantine's desire to 'please the Christian God' led to him making many decisions which altered the way Christianity was perceived by the ancient world. Constantine made huge donations to the churches in his domains. He provided new copies of the Bible, built church buildings and gave other buildings for the use of church officials. He assigned a fixed proportion of provincial revenues to church charity. He also allowed for fine and accurate copies of the Christian 'Scriptures' to be made, and he made restitution of all Christian property that had been confiscated in the persecutions.

To be a Christian was to enjoy the favour of the emperor. Joining the Christian community was no longer costly, and to accept the doctrines and adhere to the rituals was a small price to pay for the benefits that might be enjoyed.

It was during this period that many of the seeds planted by the Apostolic Fathers regarding leadership, structure and mission grew significantly and became the practice of the Church.

Leadership

A distinction between clergy and laity. The power of the leaders became immense with the creation of a distinction between leaders (the clergy) and everybody else (the laity). This power of the leaders is illustrated by an incident involving Cyprian in the third century. He was dealing with a situation in a church where a certain bishop Rogatianus was involved in a dispute with a deacon who contended against him. Cyprian told the bishop that he had the right 'according to the vigour of the episcopate and the authority of his throne' to exercise his 'priestly power' upon the 'insolent deacon'. In another letter to a certain Pupianus, he says: 'The Bishop is in the church, and the church is in the bishop; and if anyone be not with the bishop, he is not in the church.' What Cyprian says is nothing compared to what is written in the 'Apostolical Constitutions', probably in the mid to late fourth century.

> The bishop is the minister of the word, the keeper of knowledge, the mediator between God and you. After God he is your father, who has begotten you again to the adoption of sons by water and the Spirit; your ruler and governor; your king and potentate; your earthly God ... Let not the laity on all occasions trouble their governor; but let them signify their desires to him through the deacons, with whom they may be more free. For as we may not address ourselves to almighty God, but only by Christ, so let the laity make known all their desires to the bishop by the deacon, and let them act as he shall direct them ... How dare any speak against their bishop, by whom the Lord gave you the Holy Spirit through the laying on of his hands; by who ye were sealed with the oil of gladness and the unction of understanding; by whom the Lord illumined you and sent his sacred voice upon you, saying, 'Thou art my son, this day I have begotten thee.' [10]

There is so much that could be said regarding this distinction between the clergy and the laity, but most importantly, regarding its impact upon the Christian message, was that this message became the property of the clergy – they were viewed as 'the keepers of the knowledge'. For everybody else, it was not required that they have a living faith of their own, merely that they obey the leaders and conform to the customs of the Church.

Structure of meetings

We saw above how the structure of meetings changed drastically. Reality was replaced with ritual as those who attended Christian meetings became increasingly passive. The 'people' contributed less and less as the clergy became the doers of the Christian faith and everybody else had only to observe the rituals.

Mission

Salvation is found in the Church – not in Christ. The outcome of the process outlined in the previous pages was devastating to the message and mission of Jesus. Beginning with the Fathers and culminating in the reign of Constantine, Jesus and His message were lost. Now in an age of 'Acceptable Christianity', going to church and obeying its rules and conforming to its customs became the way to earn salvation. The Church, not Jesus and His grace, became perceived as the means of salvation! The priests now administered what was necessary for salvation. The free gift of grace, given as a transforming agent for all, had been forgotten. 'Its own conception of itself was altering from a communion of saints to that of an agency for salvation' (Williston Walker).[11]

This is underlined by F.F. Bruce. He quotes Origen: 'No one can have God for his Father who has not the church for his mother.'

So the Church had become the means of salvation and entry into the kingdom of God – a reward for being a faithful Christian who attended the services, recited the rituals and obeyed the clergy.

Faith in Jesus was now expressed as an external observance of ritual rather than an internal change of heart. And the structures and mission strategies that were put into place, which were to dominate for the next 1,000 years or so, with some wonderful exceptions, did little to communicate to the world the true message of Jesus and the apostles.

And then ...

6

The Reformation –
the message is rediscovered

Then ... came the Reformation.

As William Cunningham states, 'The Reformation from Popery in the sixteenth century was the greatest event, or series of events, that has occurred since the close of the canon of scripture.' [1]

The thousand or so years that unfolded following the formulation of the Christian message at Nicea tell a story of a Church that became decreasingly like the community that Jesus had intended. His message that had been so zealously protected by the apostles became almost unrecognisable as the Church became a vast imperial institution.

Cunningham again states:

> Some aspects of the development of Christianity in the Roman world from the time of Constantine onwards are none too pleasant. Time and again in the review of these years we have to record an unhappy precedent. The evident patronage extended to Christianity by the ruling power made Christianity popular in an undesirable sense. Christian leaders were tempted to exploit the influential favour they enjoyed, even when it meant subordinating the cause of justice to the apparent interests of their religion. On the other hand, they were inclined to allow the secular power too much control in church affairs, even if it was by way of gratitude for the imperial good will. Where church leaders were able to exercise political as well as spiritual authority, they did not enjoy any marked immunity from the universally corrupting tendency of power – a tendency which presents an even more displeasing spectacle in Christians than it does in other people, because it clashes so with the first principles

of Christianity. We see in those centuries the emergence of worldly ecclesiastics on the one hand, balanced by the inordinate extremities of asceticism on the other. We see nationalist animosities interfering with the proper exercise of Christian duty, to the point where national groups professing Christianity wage fierce war upon each other. We see the ugly spirit of intolerance not only directed against non-Christians but also against Christians of divergent beliefs or practices; we even see some Christians invoking against others the aid of the imperial state which but lately had persecuted all Christians alike. We see an unreasonable insistence on uniformity in non-essential matters, such as the fixing of the date of Easter and even more unimportant things than that. We see spiritual liberty hampered by a steady increase of centralised control and organisation.[2]

His summary makes depressing reading. The message of Jesus was corrupted by power-seeking leaders, concealed behind a whole raft of unhelpful and unnecessary customs and rules, and buried beneath a physical and spiritual monument.

This institution that had concealed the transforming message of Jesus and replaced it with a message that required people to conform to its doctrine and practice could not survive in the changing world of the sixteenth century. Enough was enough! The world was changing rapidly and if the Church were to continue it would have to change as well.

The world of the Reformation

Leonard Cowie, in *The Reformation*, briefly explains the huge intellectual and social shifts that were taking place during the sixteenth century: 'The paths trodden by the footsteps of ages were broken up; old things were passing away, and the faith and the life of ten centuries was dissolving like a dream.'[3]

These familiar paths were being broken because the ways that people understood the world were changing. New technology enabled people to see things differently, to question inherited assumptions and to share their thoughts and views with a much wider audience. Truth ceased to be the property of the priests and the Church, who could no longer enjoy their status as 'keepers of the knowledge'. Ordinary people, the laity, were increasingly able to find out things for themselves.

This led to new challenges and new opportunities for the Church.

Challenges from outside the Church

The Renaissance – denial of traditional authority

The world was changing during the years approaching the fifteenth century. Renaissance thinkers were no longer happy merely to accept the assumptions of the past 1,000 years and they began to ask new questions. They were not happy to accept that things were true just because the Church said so. They wanted to explore and find things out for themselves. This new way of looking at things was made possible by technological advances.

Technological advance

A new universe

It must have been an amazing time to have been alive. New things were being discovered that had never before been imagined. Think how it must have felt for the first scientists, in the fifteenth century, who looked through the newly constructed telescopes and saw, before their eyes, a vastly different universe from the one that previous generations had thought was there. The questions it caused them to ask, saw medieval assumptions concerning the earth and its place in the universe swept aside.

Books, books and more books

Imagine what it must have been like to be able to go out and buy a book, or read an article for the first time. My eldest son, as a teenager, loved to go the large bookshop in town, drink coffee and read book after book. He could not have begun to imagine what it must have been like to live at a time when reading was only available to a small number of professional clergy. Nor can people today who read newspapers and magazines, and form their opinions and views about anything from sport to who should be the next president of the United States.

Today we take reading for granted, but the social upheaval caused by the invention of the printing press was to lead to nothing short of a social revolution. When one of the first printing presses was set up in Mainz, Germany, in 1450 nobody could have imagined how revolutionary the consequences would be. Now hundreds of books could be copied in a few days; the days of copying by hand were over. Books and articles became accessible to a 'mass audience', consequently there was a new and widespread growth of education amongst laymen. It was no longer only the clergy who were educated.

By 1500, books were no longer scarce and expensive. Laymen could buy them and read the writings of the scholars for themselves. This led to people forming their own opinions rather than accepting Church doctrine as truth that must never be questioned.

This new knowledge now available to the masses of ordinary people made it more difficult for the Church to expect people to conform to its belief and practices without question. In a world where people were now thinking for themselves and forming opinions that were based upon and made available by new technological discoveries, faith in Jesus would need to be redefined. The Church could no longer continue in the way it had. Its beliefs were under scrutiny and its practice increasingly irrelevant to people who would not merely accept things uncritically.

The challenge to the Church was not an organised mutiny. It was the inevitable result of changes that were taking place in society. Ways of 'being church' that were shaped in the third and fourth centuries could not continue in a world where people would no longer just do as they were told. This, it seems, is always the case. New technology is not invented in order to undermine the Church. It is invented because it helps people to do things more effectively or more efficiently. But, repeatedly, new technology has a wider impact than the immediate purpose for which it was invented. New technology often leads to new ways of looking at the world, new habits, even new values, and it frequently presents new challenges. The new challenges that technological advance presented to the Church in the sixteenth century could have signalled the end for the Church had it merely turned a blind eye and just carried on as it had always done, but it didn't.

New challenges – new opportunities

The challenges presented by the changing world led to change within the Church. The vast increase in the power and influence of the written and spoken word had resulted in the birth of a new era. A whole new culture was being born.

Changes in learning and communication were unprecedented and the Church harnessed the dominant and most powerful influence – the written word – and in so doing rediscovered the message of Jesus and that salvation is found in Him alone, not in the Church! The rediscovery of the message resulted in changes to the method.

The new discoveries and advances in technology led many inside the Church to ask new and fundamental questions. Many began to look back beyond the traditions of the Church and to study the New Testament in Greek, the original language in which it had been written. These scholars began to discover that the biblical and Early Church writings made no mention of popes, bishops and monks, in fact there seemed to be little justification for much of what the Church did. It became clear to some that things had to change. The future could not be a continuation of the past. The Church was at a key moment in history.

This moment was grasped by a Augustinian monk, born in Saxony in 1483 – Martin Luther.

As with so many that God has used in remarkable ways, Luther was not seeking to make a name for himself. He did what he felt was the right thing to do. As Roland Bainton says of him: '… he was like a man climbing in the darkness a winding staircase in the steeple of an ancient cathedral. In the blackness he reached out to steady himself, and his hand laid hold of a rope. He was startled to hear the clanging of a bell.' [4]

Luther the reformer

Like many of his contemporaries, Luther studied Greek. These studies led him to question the assumptions of the medieval Church. He especially questioned the special place of the clergy and the sacraments as the means of salvation. He discovered in the writings of Paul that 'Man is justified by faith alone'.

> Night and day I pondered until I saw the connection between the justice of God and the statement that 'the just shall live by his faith'. Then I grasped that the justice of God is that righteousness by which through grace and sheer mercy God justifies us through faith. Thereupon I felt myself to be reborn and to have gone through open doors into paradise. The whole of Scripture took on a new meaning, and whereas before the 'justice of God' had filled me with hate, now it became to me inexpressibly sweet in greater love. This passage of Paul became to me a gate to heaven ...[5]

It was this discovery of the true, life-transforming message of Jesus that prompted Luther to do something that would change things. As he read the Scriptures and then observed the Church, he became angry that so much of what happened seemed contrary to the message of the Bible. What he then did, although he had not intended it to, caused what is probably best described as a Christian revolution.

Following what was the usual practice of his day, Luther posted 95 theses on the door of the castle church in Wittenberg. His theses attacked the 'indulgences'. The Church taught that it was possible to buy sinners out of purgatory. As an excerpt from a sermon by the Dominican monk Tetzel demonstrates: 'As soon as the coin in the coffer rings. The soul from purgatory springs.'

But there was more. Luther went on to deny that the pope had power over purgatory, God, not the pope, was the judge of eternal issues, and sinners were not saved by payment but only by God's mercy.

There is no doubt that Luther was raising some fundamental issues which in previous days might never have been seriously discussed. However, now there was the printing press!

His theses were translated and copied and copied and copied. In a way that could never have happened before, issues of what the Church taught and how it should be led were discussed in the open – the people joined in the debate – Luther's 95 theses became the talk of Germany!

The message

In a world where the authority of the Church was seriously doubted, Luther and others who followed him, reminded the world that it was the Bible, not the traditions of the Church, which contained the authoritative message of Jesus. Salvation comes through faith not by observing rituals. Luther was restating the message of Jesus and the apostles. He saw that this message had been lost, that the Church had departed from the message of God's gift of grace as the basis for faith. Commenting on Paul's letter to the Romans, he writes: 'The sum and substance of this letter is: to pull down, to pluck up, and to destroy all wisdom and righteousness of the flesh and to affirm and enlarge (prove to be large) the reality of sin, however unconscious we may be of its existence.' [6]

For Luther, the problem with all people, whether Jew or Gentile, was that we all have a belief in an inner goodness. There is something within all of us that believes that somehow we can, by our religious observance and effort, earn the reward of grace. He comments: 'For God does not want to save us by our own but by an extraneous righteousness, one that does not originate in ourselves but comes to us from beyond ourselves, which does not arise on earth but comes from Heaven.'

Luther restated what Paul had said concerning grace:

$$\text{Grace} \longrightarrow \text{faith} + \text{love!}$$

Having rediscovered this message it was important that it was heard. It needed to be communicated. In a world where the dominant method of communication was the word, the message of Jesus began to be defined in terms of 'the Word of God'. The Scriptures and the New Testament formed this 'Word' and this was the message that the Church had to communicate.

The movement spreads

What Luther began was carried on by others. Many began to experience God and see things in a new way. The movement spread across Europe and reached into England.

A wonderful story of the difference this rediscovery of the message of Jesus was making is that of Thomas Bilney. Bilney was key in creating the reforming group in Cambridge. In 1527 he wrote a letter to Bishop Tunstall of London. His letter contained his heartfelt condemnation of those to whom he had offered his confession: these priests 'sought rather their own gain than the salvation of my sick and languishing soul', he said, but then continued to tell how, in spite of all of this, he came to meet with Jesus.

> But at last I heard speak of Jesus, even when the New Testament was first set forth by Erasmus ... I chanced upon this sentence of St Paul (O most and comfortable sentence to my soul!) in 1 Timothy 1: 'It is a true saying, and worthy of all men to be embraced, that Christ Jesus came into the world to save sinners, of whom I am the chief and principal.' This one sentence, through God's instruction and inward working, which I did not then perceive, did so exhilarate my heart, before being wounded with the guilt of my sins, and being almost in despair, that immediately I felt a marvellous comfort and quietness, insomuch that my bruised bones leaped for joy.
>
> After this, the Scripture began to be more pleasant to me than the honey or the honey-comb; wherein I learned that all my travails, all my fasting and watching, all the redemption of masses and pardons, being done without trust in Christ, who only saveth his people from their sins; these, I say, I learned to be nothing else but even (as St Augustine saith) a hasty and swift running out of the right way.

It was this rediscovery of the message of Jesus that led to what we call the Reformation – literally the reforming of a large part of the Church, this reformation was in protest against much of what was considered wrong in the Church of its day. Hence it became known as the Protestant Reformation and those churches that reformed became known as Protestant churches.

As always, there is a relationship between what the Church believes (the message), and what the Church does (the method). The Reformation emphasis on the message of Jesus being contained in the Bible and not in the traditions of the Church had huge implications for what happened when Christians met together. The role of the leadership and the structure of the meetings were drastically changed.

The method

Leadership

A significant change was in the leadership. The reformed churches believed that the message of Jesus was contained in the written word of the Bible. Jesus was therefore to be encountered by people as they heard the Word of God. As such, priests were not required, but preachers. The Word of God must be heard so it must be preached, therefore the key function of the leader of a reformed church was to preach.

The preacher was not a 'priest' but God's spokesman: 'Ministers are ambassadors of God, and speak in Christ's stead. If they preach what is founded on the Scriptures, their word, as far as it is agreeable to the mind of God, is considered as God's.'[7]

This emphasis on preaching had implications for the structure of the meetings as well. The changes were far reaching.

Structure of meeting

Church buildings were altered. The altar was moved and replaced by a pulpit. This demonstrated that God is encountered through His Word, not through the ritual or the altar, because, as John Stott points out:

> For the sake of the proclaimed word the world exists with all of its words. In the sermon the foundation for a new world is laid. Here the original word becomes audible. There is no evading or getting away from the spoken word of the sermon, nothing releases us from the necessity of

this witness, not even cult or liturgy … The preacher should be assured that Christ enters the congregation through those words which he proclaims from the Scripture.[8]

Pulpits, being placed in the centre, and being the focal point of the church service, underlined the importance placed on preaching the Word. But they were also very practical. The preacher raised high in the air could be seen, and in the days before Public Address systems, heard as well.

Congregation
It wasn't only the role of the leaders that changed. Those in the congregation had the responsibility to listen to the Word of God being preached.

Summary

During the sixteenth century the Church went through a period of huge change. As a result the message of Jesus and the apostles began to be communicated once again and many of those who attended church out of tradition were awakened to a new realisation of what this message really was. Many changes were made to church structures, roles and buildings, all in order to facilitate the communication of the Christian message.

The Reformation was huge in its impact. It spread across Europe and then in later years into the 'new worlds' that were being discovered. The Reformers had seized the moment that was offered; by grasping the opportunities offered by the changing world in which they lived.

From message to method

7

So, the message of Jesus, the answer to the question 'Who's the bloke on the wall?' has been through a process of being diluted, polluted and then rediscovered. But the Reformation in the sixteenth century did not signal the end of the story. It is part of a process that continues to move in cycles.

The diagram below simply presents this process or cycle.

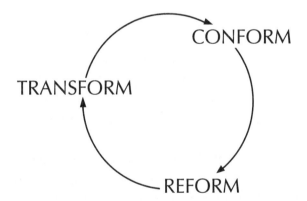

The story from the Reformation onwards is one where at different times individuals, or small groups of people, have felt that the Church has not been communicating the message in the right way, so something new has begun. These new expressions which over a period of time have become significant enough to be called denominations began in response to a perceived inadequacy in the Church of their day. Each emphasised a particular aspect of the faith that seemed to be missing.

It is fascinating to observe that each of these new movements passed through the same cycle. Much of the life and vitality of the early days of the movements was slowly replaced with a structure and order to which those belonging to the movement were expected to conform. Eventually, their original aim became buried under a new kind of liturgy and structure. What has been true of movements since the Reformation can also be said of most local churches.

It becomes clear that this cycle is somehow inevitable. There is something about us as people. We contribute something that means it will always be so. It is not possible to point to a time in history, or to a particular group and say that they are the ones to blame. The challenge to retain the pure message of Jesus and communicate it in relevant ways has continued since the time of Jesus Himself. The question we need to consider is where are we in this cycle? Before we look at this in Part Three, I want to go into a little more detail concerning the process.

Transform

This is the visionary or pioneering phase of the movement or church.

Movements begin in order to change things. By their very nature they are introduced to achieve something that is not already being achieved. Movements are therefore about revolution or change. They exist to bring about transformation.

During the initial stages of the movement, a leader or small group of leaders have a clear sense of vision to achieve a specific goal. These visionary leaders are concerned, above everything else, to ensure that this vision is realised. It is the vision that is paramount and all the activity that takes place and the structures that are put into place are in order that the vision will be realised. None of the things that the movement does are ends in themselves but the means by which the end, or the vision, will be achieved.

Means and ends

In order for the various activities to be effective in achieving the vision certain structures are put into place. They are not the end! Their value is not in themselves but only inasmuch as they help to make the vision become a reality.

In the 'transform' phase, the purpose of the movement or local church is relatively clear: communicate the message of Jesus, keep it pure and help people to come to know and believe this message.

During this phase the church will probably contain many of the following features:

- A leadership that is committed to empowering, encouraging and enabling believers to transform the world, whatever the obstacles.
- Meeting together is dynamic, in the sense that the meeting is not an end in itself. As a result of meeting together believers are enthused, encouraged and equipped to put their faith into practice. Those who meet are renewed and transformed. There is not a rigid liturgy or certain set time when 'acts of worship' must take place.
- Mission is effective because those who belong to the movement or church are being continually renewed and transformed within the community. They don't feel isolated but part of something important.

The result of this dynamic approach to all that is done is that the church or movement grows. This is, in some ways, a mixed blessing. Of course it is a real blessing because it is the very thing that the movement intends, it is why it exists, but the inevitable 'success' brings its own challenges. As the movement grows, it begins to develop an identity of its own and, subtly and inevitably, those things that were put into place as a means, begin to become the end in themselves and the movement that existed to 'transform' stumbles, or drifts into a period where it is best typified by an expectation that people will conform.

Conform

It is sadly inevitable that after a period that is best defined as transformation, a phase begins where conformity is the dominant feature. That which began to change things has now put into place new ways of achieving the aims of the movement. I want to explore five features of this phase.

Means and ends

What was put in place in order to achieve the aims of the vision, the means, now becomes that which those within the group do regardless of whether or not it achieves the original end, what is done becomes an end in itself. We do it just because we have always done it! The time and energy of those within the group become geared to preservation rather than pioneering.

So why does this always happen, and what are its implications?

Organisation is necessary and inevitable

As the movement spreads it is not possible for the original leaders to take responsibility for all that happens. Responsibility has to be delegated, and consequently new leaders are appointed.

In addition, the growing movement has to be organised. Problems have to be overcome and people need to know what they are doing. Structures are put into place to properly instruct those in the movement in its values and to know what is expected of them as 'members'.

This 'organising' is a necessary part of the process as it does begin to create order and shape. Those within the movement or church know where they stand, and what is expected of them.

But slowly the 'organising' develops into 'an organisation'. Things which were originally done 'in order to' achieve the aims of the church or movement, begin to be done, not necessarily because they are effective, but because that is how the organisation does things.

Slowly, the activities and structures begin to become the end in themselves as the organisation begins to have its own identity, and increasingly it is this, not the vision itself, that is served. The power of this cannot be over-estimated. This sense of identity can become so strong that those who have belonged to the organisation or church for a long time will make huge sacrifices just to keep it going even if it has long since failed to achieve the purpose for which it was begun. But it is not only the need for order and structure. It is also because all movements, organisations and churches are made up of people. And people, even Christians, retain a great deal of self-interest whichever group they join or belong to.

The problem of self-interest

It is this feature, perhaps more than any other, that we don't really like to talk about or apply to ourselves. We know that Jesus accused the Pharisees and religious leaders of it and the Church after the apostles became riddled with it. We may look at others in the Church today and 'blame' them for it. But the problem is not restricted to any time within the history of the Church or any group within the Church today. It is a problem we all have, no one is immune. All of us, by nature, like things to be the way we like them!

A number of years ago I was pastor of a church. Over a couple of years lots of new people were reached, people with little or no church background, and many of them came to faith in Jesus, were baptised and became members of the church. Because these people had no church background they were not familiar with all that went on in the church. The existing members were very familiar with it – they liked it. The new believers were not trying to be difficult when they were critical of the way things were done. They just could not see how what happened in the church really helped it to achieve what it said it was about. And most of what it did didn't help the new believers very much. The style of teaching and worship suited those who were familiar with it but was not appropriate for people who had never been to church. So I changed a number of things. Instead of preaching a sermon at every service, where everybody sat and listened, we had open discussion, where people could ask their questions rather than never have them answered.

I remember one deacons' meeting. It was significant because it took place at a key time. For the first time since I had become pastor of the church, the number of new people who were in membership was now greater than the number of people that had been in membership when I arrived. For want of a better expression, the balance of power had shifted to the new people and they could vote to change things. This made some of the deacons a little nervous. I remember discussing with the deacons some of the changes that were being made to help these new believers. One of the deacons became quite upset, looked me in the face, and said, 'You're ruining our church.' I must say I was a little bit taken aback and, as a young man new to leadership, I was disappointed that there seemed 'little rejoicing' at the sinners coming to know the Lord.

I would guess you're interested to know what happened next. Having overcome that knot that comes in the stomach at certain times, I said, in as gracious a way as I could muster, 'I appreciate what you've said and know it must be difficult for you to see everything changing. But the problem is, it is not your church, and it isn't mine, it belongs to Jesus and we need to do what He wants.'

I've often thought back to that occasion; in some ways it was a key point for me. I saw lived out before my own eyes a situation that was just like, though on a much smaller scale, what happened at the Council in Jerusalem as they discussed the situation at Antioch. 'The new people are not conforming to the way that we do things and they should.'

This 'self-interest' – wanting it to be the way we like it – is a huge contributory factor to the emergence of the requirement that people conform to 'our way of doing it' before they can join us. 'We like it this way' is often the reason that we continue to do things in the way that we do them. Unfortunately when this becomes the reason that we do things it signals the end of transformation and the beginning of conformity. Pioneering ceases and preservation becomes our motive.

This may sound a bit extreme but I think, when it comes down to it, it is a fairly common thing. As an evangelist I have frequently over the years been asked to lead missions with churches. I always ask why the church wants to do the mission. The answer most frequently given is that they want more people to come to church. I can understand this, but it should not be our motivation. It should be that we want people to discover Jesus.

But what is it that causes us to like things the way they are even if, deep down, we know they are not achieving what they used to? Probably the answer to this question is that we find comfort in the familiar, and it is easier to continue with what we are doing than to try something else.

Helpful additions become inevitable substitutes

I owe this phrase to my college principal, Dr Raymond Brown, who always made church history come alive in such an interesting and helpful way. He used this phrase to explain how what is put into place to help the movement eventually becomes that which the movement continues to do long after it is helpful. These helpful additions may be doctrinal or practical.

A good example of how this happens is an issue to which we referred earlier. You may remember the outrage of Luther at the indulgences. It is hard to imagine how the Church ever reached the stage where it believed that souls could be bought from purgatory by putting money into the offertory. It began as a helpful addition that was never intended to result in any idea of souls being bought out of purgatory. During the rise of the Barbarians, Roman soldiers were being massacred. The pope at the time, Gregory the Great, in the face of such grief among Roman citizens, sought to comfort them by suggesting that those who had departed might still reach heaven, so it would be good to pray for them. This is not the teaching of Jesus, but it was 'added' in order to offer pastoral comfort to distressed believers. But over time this helpful addition became a substitute for truth and what was intended to be helpful became a vehicle for exploitation.

But it is not only doctrine that can become a substitute for the truth; so can practice. Things are put into place, or added, because at the time they are an appropriate way of the movement achieving its goal. A good example is pulpits. As we saw, these were put in place of altars at the time of the Reformation because, doctrinally, it was in the Word not the sacrament that the believer encountered Christ. This Word therefore had to be heard and pulpits, because they were elevated and placed in the middle of the church building, enabled the words to be heard. It is the hearing of the Word, not the physical construction of a pulpit, that is the helpful addition. However, in many churches it was the physical pulpit itself that became the inevitable substitute and there are many Christians still, who feel it is inappropriate to preach from anywhere other than the pulpit, even if the church now has a good PA system.

These helpful additions are often 'added' because through them God moves in remarkable ways and brings about remarkable transformation. Consequently those within the movement are so convinced of their importance that, as time passes, they and their descendants seek to preserve them even though they are no longer effective. They become 'sacraments', things that are associated with the intervention of God, and it is felt that the preservation, or continuance of doing things in the way they were once done, will somehow bring about the results that were once achieved.

But this doesn't happen. These moments of God's intervention are remembered, and become part of the 'ritual' of the church. Increasingly those who come afterwards, people who have not experienced the intervention of God that led to the ritual being introduced in the first place, seek only to preserve the ritual because in the memory of the church or movement it is associated with the intervention of God. Ritual has replaced reality, the helpful addition has become the inevitable substitute, the means has become the end. That which was put into place to help now becomes a hindrance, because the energy spent preserving it prevents those within the church from investing in the future.

The membership changes

As time passes, the requirements for membership in the movement or church change. Those who joined the movement originally were converted to the movement and made a conscious decision to join. The children of these converts may not be so much converted to it as socialised or educated into it. In succeeding generations those who join the movement may have no experience of the church or movement in its pioneering days. All they have experienced is the need for preservation. Membership, for them, is less about transformation and more about faithfully observing the customs. Consequently, the expectations that the church or movement places upon the members are very different; at its simplest they are expected to turn up at meetings to show their support.

Summary

As a result of this process the purpose of the church becomes less to do with seeking transformation in the lives of people, rather it anticipates that people will conform to its message and practices without the need for transformation. Increasingly, during this phase, salvation becomes the property of the church to such an extent that, as we saw earlier, the church imposes upon people a range of practices that are unrecognisable in the message of Jesus.

During this phase:

- Leadership is committed to teaching the faith and defending what is thought to be orthodoxy. In addition, leadership ceases to empower people to live transformed and transforming lives, rather it creates a dependence upon itself.
- The leader becomes primarily concerned with looking after the people at the church, rather than leading them out into the world. Consequently, ordinary believers become passive spectators rather than active participants.
- Meeting together loses a clear purpose. It has become a custom or habit and Christians meet because that is what is expected, regardless of whether their meeting together is achieving anything. The style of the 'meeting' becomes more passive, and it is rigid in its feel, only taking place at set times, in special places and it will often require that a member of the clergy leads the 'act of worship'.

Mission may still be regarded as important but it rarely takes place. The language of mission is used, but the reality is that few people from outside of the group that normally meet together, come to faith in Jesus.

Everything has become institutionalised and as Derek Tidball helpfully points out: 'Institutionalisation refers to structures, however, when they have ceased to function in the best interests of the movement they are supposedly serving.'[1]

This short parable may help:

Mike and Sally, Paul and Jean, Jim, John and Christine, lived in Liverton. Each of them had come to know Jesus in a personal way but the church they went to frustrated them. There seemed to be little they could do to encourage those within the church to reach out to others. Jim lived above a fish and chip shop in the middle of town. He, like the others, felt that it would be good for them to meet together and pray for each other, and that God would work through them to reach out to others.

They didn't want to be divisive, just effective. They found their meetings together really useful. They met at times that were most convenient for them all, bearing in mind their family and work commitments. They prayed and shared about what really mattered. Jim led, Sally played the guitar, and Paul and Jean were great at hospitality. The support and encouragement they received from meeting together gave them the courage and desire to share their faith with other people. So they started talking to their friends and neighbours about Jesus and some came to know Him and joined in their meetings above the chip shop. Eventually more and more people joined them and great as this was it caused them a problem; Jim's flat was no longer big enough – close fellowship does not mean sitting on top of one another. As a result they decided they would have to meet somewhere else, so they started meeting at the community centre. There were about 30 of them by now. The move to the community centre was interesting. Because the space was bigger and there were more people, the style of their meetings changed. They became more formal. Also they had to meet at the same time each week because of the hiring of the hall. Jim was joined in leadership by Paul and Christine; they had started the church so it seemed natural that they should become leaders. Still the church grew, and then something began to happen. There were now over 60 people that were part of the church. They looked at some of the other established churches in the town and saw that they had their own building and a full-time minister. It would be nice to have a building of their own, a proper church, and to call it something. It would also be great to have a minister, someone who was trained and who could do the job properly.

As they met and prayed together they were unaware that the content of their prayers had changed since the chip-shop days. Then their constant prayer had been that each of them would win others for the Lord. They still prayed for this but now, with 60 people coming, with young people and children to think of, most of their praying was for the money to buy a building and employ a minister.

Eventually their opportunity came, a plot of land became available. After a huge fund-raising drive they built a proper church with a cross on it and everything. Now the church had become a real church, they even gave it a name; they called it Liverton Family Church. Now they were a real church they wanted to do things properly, like other churches. To accomplish this they needed more worship leaders, more leaders for the church, some to look after the buildings, some to look after the young people. They also needed a treasurer and a secretary. Their meeting together changed; now they were a real church they wanted to do what real churches do, their meetings were now mainly songs and sermons. Then they were able to afford a minister and people thought that he would take away a lot of the pressure that had been on them. The minister preached at each of the services because that is what he was paid to do. The church still talked about reaching the community, they still used the same language they had always used and they still prayed for the town but, without noticing, they now prayed that people would join 'the church' rather than meet Jesus. They talked about 'the church' a lot now, almost as if it had an identity of its own. You would have thought it had, because now it had a building it had headed paper and at the top of each sheet was a picture of the church building. Unfortunately those within the church had become so preoccupied with church that they began to lose touch with people outside. Their prayers became much more general, led from the front, the church prayed for the town, but opportunities for specific and honest prayer largely disappeared. Prayers tended to be for 'them' as a group rather than individuals by name.

More time passed and the children of the founding members, now grown up, had become parents themselves; there were now about 100 people in the church. They really appreciated all that they had received from the church and were committed to making sure that it continued to grow, and during the next few years it really grew. Many of the children of church members came to faith and new people joined. These were mostly from other churches, only a very few from outside, but that didn't matter – there were so many within, the church would survive now anyway. After ten more years it reached 250 members and everybody was thrilled at the way that God was blessing the church. Unfortunately none of those baptised in the last five years were from outside!

Now the church was so busy that most of the ministry and financial resources were taken up with running the church, so continual mission got lost. However the church did have a mission once in a while because it knew deep down that it existed to reach its community – it had just become so busy being a church. They still talked about reaching people for Jesus but they also wanted to have a full and lively church because, if they were honest, it made them feel better.

The long-term future of Liverton Family church was now pretty assured. It had lots of people coming to it, and ways of doing things that were pleasing to those who came. It proudly continued to do things the right way, the way it had always done them, and this pleased most of those who came.

But as time passed, the way that the church did things became dated and not so relevant to the people now living in their town. But they had become so accustomed to doing what they did and, to be honest, they had a feeling that the way they did things is the way they should be done. Many of the meetings they had set up years ago were no longer achieving what they were set up for but the people who went enjoyed them, so they were kept going. The church was in decline now but nobody really noticed because it was still fairly full and over the years it had built up enough reserves to keep afloat.

Now we have reached today and people within the church are beginning to raise questions about what the church does and why it does them. There seems to be no reason except that this is how they have always done them. What will happen next? It all depends. The future for this church, like any church is not inevitable.

It could carry on as it is and ignore the change around it. Death would be slow because it is large and financially secure.

Or it could change and reach new people as they used to when they were above the chip shop. It could move into a necessary phase for any organisation that wants to overcome the inevitable tendency that leads to 'conform'. It could reform.

Reform

If the movement or church is to continue, it must move on to the reform phase. God does not give up on His people; He raises up leaders who can do nothing other than remind the church of what it should be. As a result the church 'reforms'. This phase will inevitably contain some conflict as accepted ways of doing things will need to be changed. Some will accept this gladly, others will fight against it with all their might, many will be somewhere in the middle.

During this phase:

- Leadership is primarily concerned with helping the church and individuals to rediscover the purpose behind who we are and what we do. Leaders will know the stress and anxiety of trying to help this process take place most effectively.
- Meeting together has a purpose again. Those who meet discuss how they may rediscover the vision rather than merely continue to do the same thing. This is exhilarating for some and daunting for others.
- Mission becomes transformational as the church remembers that it is the transforming message of Jesus, not an expectation that people will conform to church. That it exists to communicate. The transformation begins with those in the church and as they are transformed they discover a new desire and ability to transform others.

In some instances the first stage of mission may be the people who currently attend church. It is not inconceivable that a large proportion of those within church are those who have been socialised or educated into church rather than converted to Jesus. It may be that their devotion is to the 'inevitable substitutes' rather than God Himself. During a time of reformation, mission begins with the church. This does not mean that those who have been at the church are suddenly condemned and blamed. They have in many ways preserved things so that at least a Christian community still exists. They should be helped to experience more!

We live at a time to reform. A time that will include tension, but a time of great opportunity. The message of Jesus does and will transform lives of people living in the twenty-first century, but first they have to know what it is. For that to happen we need to get rid of many of the 'inevitable substitutes' that have been added to the message and to which we become so accustomed and somehow expect people to conform. We need to remove these so that people can once again see the pure transparent message of Jesus. So that once again the message of Jesus will transform us, and through us transform the world.

PART 3

The Method

8

Change for good

'If you put a frog in water and slowly heat it, the frog will eventually let itself be boiled to death. We, too, will not survive if we don't respond to the radical way in which the world is changing,' writes Charles Handy, a prolific author on the subject of change, not in the Church, but in society. These words appear on the cover of his book *The Age of Unreason*.

We live at a time when the changes that are taking place in society dwarf any previous times of change. In the midst of ever-improving technologies, new discoveries, changing values and beliefs, a change that is here to stay is that people no longer attend church out of custom or habit as they did in the past. Those days are gone, and while this may sound depressing, it actually provides us with a remarkable opportunity. It provides us with the opportunity to reform.

We live at a time when the Church will reach people as it demonstrates that faith in Jesus makes a positive difference to our lives. People today are interested in things that work before they will ask if they are true. If we ignore this and continue to do what we have always done without recognising that everything around us is changing, then the Church, like the frog, will slowly reach a point where it no longer exists. But it is my belief that this will never happen. This is not a time to be depressed, it is time to grasp the opportunity.

Consider the following two contrasting quotes:

New ways of thinking about familiar things can release new energies and make all manner of things possible. (Charles Handy, *Age of Unreason*)

If you always do what you've always done, you'll always get what you've always got. (Sue Knight, international business consultant and author)

Grasping the opportunity afforded by the changing world will require that the Church does things differently, that it reforms. The fundamental change that must be grasped is that the Church can no longer expect people to come along and conform. If people have somehow 'got the message' that church is for religious people and they are not religious, we must go to them and help them to see that the message of Jesus is very different to what they think.

This change, if taken seriously, will have implications for everything we do, but it is important to note that the challenge of our day is not merely to change. The challenge or opportunity of our day is that we become effective in reaching people with the good news about Jesus. Change is only the means to that end, it is not something that should happen for its own sake.

So change is not a choice, it is inevitable; the question is, what is good change? Many Christians I have met accept that we live at a time of change but still hope that those outside the Church will somehow decide to change the way they live and come to church. It is extremely unlikely that a boy who asks, 'Who's the bloke on the wall?' is ever likely just to start coming to church. We cannot anticipate or hope that the change for the good will happen outside, it must begin with us.

A great old favourite book of mine, first published in 1908, has the title *What Will it Take to Change the World?* The introduction contains a little sentence that is so simple yet so challenging and important: 'The warm enthusiasm of grateful love must burn in the heart and drive all the life.'

The world will be changed for the better as God's people are changed. Transformed people can transform the world – it has to start with us, and it is happening. All over, churches are beginning to wake from their slumber and, motivated by their love for Jesus, are beginning to remove the inevitable substitutes and are sharing with lost people the message that Jesus loves them just as they are.

It is as this continues, as Christians live transformed lives, not behind closed doors but 'in the open', that people will get the real message of Jesus as opposed to the counterfeit message many somehow have picked up.

A helpful way of considering how things have changed, and must change, is by taking on board the reality that Europe, once the centre of Christianity, is now a mission field. Churches are surrounded by people who have never heard the gospel, and who would never dream of conforming to a set of customs and traditions that are alien to them.

An excerpt from a speech made by Chief Otetani in 1805 makes this point so well. It sheds some light on how people will be reached in a missionary context. Otetani was the chief of the Seneca tribe. Born in 1758, he became known as Red Jacket, from the bright red coat given him by the British when he supported them during the American Revolution.

Red Jacket's speech was made at a council of chiefs in response to Christian missionaries trying to baptise his followers.[1] The whole eloquent speech is worth reading but I have included just the key points. He said:

> There was a time when our forefathers owned this great island. Their seats extended from the rising to the setting sun. The Great Spirit had made it for the use of Indians. He had created the buffalo, the deer, and other animals for food … But an evil day came upon us. Your forefathers crossed the great water and landed on this island. Their numbers were small. They found friends and not enemies. They told us they had fled from their own country for fear of wicked men and had come here to enjoy their religion. They asked for a small seat. We took pity on them, granted their request, and they sat down among us. We gave them corn and meat; they gave us poison in return.

Red Jacket continued to outline how the hospitality of the Indians was abused as more and more settlers heard about this new land and came and lived there and eventually stole the land they had been welcomed to. He then moved on and accused the white man of more than taking their land: 'You have got our country, but are not satisfied; you want to force your religion upon us.'

It is the concluding words of his speech that are so poignant and relevant to any situation in which the Church is seeking to communicate the message of Jesus to people that do not want merely to conform to a set of religious customs. He concluded:

Brother, we are told that you have been preaching to the white people in this place. These people are our neighbours. We are acquainted with them. We will wait a little while and see what effect your preaching has upon them. If we find it does them good, makes them honest, and less disposed to cheat Indians, we will then consider again of what you have said.

The words of Red Jacket, spoken so long ago, presented the same challenge to the settlers as the boy in the twenty-first century presents to the Church today when he asks who the bloke on the wall is. We cannot expect people to conform to our customs and traditions. Why is what we believe any better than what they believe? We must allow God to transform our lives and then, through us, to transform others. People must see a difference in us before they will consider our message.

While this change may at one level be easy to understand, it is hard to instigate, because so much of what we currently do in churches was introduced during times when many from society regularly attended church. They believed, or perhaps a better word is 'accepted', the doctrine without necessarily encountering God. They did what was expected of them, recited the creeds and listened to the sermons. They did not need to be convinced of the truth and value of faith in Jesus before they came to church.

Those days are largely over. People now will not attend church out of a sense of it being what is expected and we can no longer expect them to merely accept and recite the doctrines of the church as true; they will need to be convinced. This will require that they encounter God in the lives of those who follow Jesus and that they come to experience Him for themselves. And this, if we are honest, is the challenge. But why not view it as an opportunity? I firmly believe that most Christians have a strong feeling that things aren't quite as they should be and that much of what we do is no longer relevant. Changing what we do will not only be a benefit to those outside, it will also benefit many Christians whose faith has become stale and lacking the meaning for which they long.

It is important to say at this stage that while I am firmly convinced there is a need for this fundamental change, I do not want to dismiss or devalue the lives and witness of many Christians who in recent generations have stood for the faith. There are so many unsung heroes who, through difficult and challenging times, have faithfully kept things going. These people should be appreciated and thanked.

I remember speaking at an event once where I learned this lesson. I had been speaking about the need for change and, without meaning to, had suggested that what had happened in the Church up until now had not hit the mark, change was needed. Following my talk an elderly lady came up, shook me by the hand and said something like this: 'I agree with all that you have said, I know we need to change and I long for people to come to know Jesus ... My skin might need ironing but I still love Him, you know. Keep challenging the Church to change but try not to forget some of us who have been labouring for years.'

So we thank those who have got us here, but we must change and continue to change. This will require that we do things differently. The key question as we begin to explore the changes that are needed, is 'What does different mean?' Two key principles must form the framework within which we seek to do things differently.

1. The message must be Jesus.
2. The method must reflect the message.

The message must be Jesus

'That's obvious', is the response that many Christians would make to this point. Many churches I have visited say to me, 'We haven't got everything right here but we do preach the gospel,' And they do, I am sure. The theology is sound and the biblical truths are preached. But in many ways that is the easy part. It is not so very difficult to preach the gospel in a context where those that come believe it already. If the message of our church is to be Jesus, then more is required than the preaching of biblical sermons. The real challenge is that the words that are spoken should be reflected in what we do.

For example, it is easy to say that Jesus came to seek and to save the lost and yet have in place a variety of habits and customs that make it difficult for lost people to find out about Him.

The method must reflect the message

You may find the following statement provocative but I am convinced not only that it is true, but that if grasped as being true and then used as a basis for doing what needs to be done, it would release churches across the world into effective evangelism.

> There is nothing that we do in church that we have to do when we do it, how we do it or where we do it. The time, method and location should be governed not by our custom but by what will be most effective in communicating the message of Jesus.

We might think about what we could change, which may include any number of things such as the time and content of the service, whether to have house groups or cells ... let's face it the list is endless. There are so many things to choose from if we are to change. But before we tinker with the activity we must consider the fundamental question – 'Why are we changing?' Again there are numerous answers that churches may give to this question but I would suggest that the most important is 'In order that our method, what we do, will reflect our message, what we believe – and that message must be the message of Jesus'.

What we do should be done differently if it is concealing rather than revealing the message of Jesus. If the additions that our church or denomination have put into place, those things which form part of our history, customs and traditions, now conceal rather than reveal the message, then they must be changed.

This sounds drastic but it is this kind of change that will help us to take the opportunity that is before us. Whichever activities your church is engaged in, you can be assured that each one is the result of an 'addition' that at some time in the past was valuable; the question must be – is it still valuable?

God has never laid down a blueprint for what a church must do. He has told us what church is for – to reach the lost. How we do it should be a response to what will be effective. This is extremely liberating, but also hard.

Theodore Roosevelt once said: 'Far better is it to dare mighty things, to win glorious triumphs – even though chequered by failure – than to rank with those poor spirits who neither enjoy much nor suffer much, because they live in a grey twilight that knows not victory nor defeat.'

Many of us feel a moving in our spirit as we read rousing words like these. We think of the church we attend, of the Jesus we love, and we long to do something, to grasp the opportunity that is before us. Unfortunately, for too many, that is as far as it has got, but now is the time for something different, now is the time for change.

Making change

Much of my thinking on this subject has been influenced by Charles Handy who has written a number of helpful books on the subject of 'managing change'. He does not write about change in the Church but in society, business and culture generally, and much of what he says is so appropriate to the opportunity we have.

In his book, *The Age of Unreason*,[2] Handy uses the term 'Discontinuous Change'. This, for him, describes the kind of change that is not just doing the same things a little bit differently, it is not 'more of the same'. He contrasts this kind of change with what he calls 'Continuous Change' which he describes as comfortable change, where our past is the guide to our future. He includes a helpful story that simply explains the difference. An American friend, visiting Britain and Europe for the first time, wondered, 'Why is it that over here whenever I ask the reason for anything, any institution or ceremony or set of rules, they always give me an historical answer – *because* ... whereas in my country we always want a functional answer – *in order to* ...' (p.3, my italics).

The difference between Continuous Change and Discontinuous Change is that the former is measured by tradition, the latter by effectiveness.

The term Discontinuous Change may be confusing or seem to have more to do with the business world than church. Consequently, what Handy calls Discontinuous Change I call 'radical discipleship'. This terminology fits better with our situation but has the same implications for us within the Church as Discontinuous Change has in society.

Radical

It is important to understand what the word radical means. It is often understood as being alternative and different, but being radical does not mean just being different for the sake of it. Radical stems from the Latin *radix* (root). To be radical therefore means to go back to the root, or the source. For us this means looking back beyond our customs and habits, those additions that have now defined how we feel church must be done. We need to go back beyond these and discover the message as given by Jesus, without the additions. It is this that must define what we do. It will liberate us to begin to do what must be done in order to achieve the primary purpose, rather than feel bound to work within a way of doing things which was once effective but is no longer.

Being radical provides the opportunity to bring about change that is not constrained by the framework of the inevitable substitutes of the past. It provides us with the opportunity to think and act beyond what has become the usual way things are done. The future need not be a continuation of the past, it can be different – it can be effective.

It is interesting that this call to be radical, to stay true to the aims of the movement, had to be impressed on Timothy who was leading the church in Ephesus. Paul wrote two letters to him. In his first, his concluding comments contain the words 'Timothy, guard what has been entrusted to your care' (1 Tim. 6:20), and in his second he writes, 'Guard the good deposit that was entrusted to you' (2 Tim. 1:14). Even in the early days of the movement leaders needed to be reminded to stay true to the original vision and not to deviate from it or become side-tracked. Paul is urging Timothy not to lose the original vision and allow it to be replaced by the traditions and structures that are only appropriate for the specific situation he is facing.

On the front cover of Charles Handy's book, *Beyond Certainty*, he states, 'We must not let our past, however glorious, get in the way of our future.'

It is understandably such a challenge to us to be radical because it is difficult not to be guided by what we have been accustomed to.

For many it will be in our local church. We may remember the founders, its glorious past. Each church has its own story to tell, its own customs and habits. Things we have inherited, that were put in place 'in order to' achieve certain things but have been done for so long that they now happen 'because' that is what we do. It is these that often provide the boundaries within which we operate.

The opportunity we have requires that we remove these boundaries and discover again how to communicate the message of Jesus in ways that will reach people today rather than people living at the time our church was founded.

It is, though, more complicated than just the local church of which we are part. As well as having its own history, each church is part of a group of other churches that has its own history. This wider group, or denomination, will, like our individual church, have its stories to tell, its customs and habits, its glorious past. It has ways of doing things that were put in place 'in order to' achieve certain things. But again, these have now become things that are done 'because' doing them in this way demonstrates that our church is being a good example of what a church in our denomination should be like. This again provides the boundaries within which we operate.

Each denomination, or stream of churches, as with each local expression of the Church, must seek to remove the boundaries, and help and equip churches to reach people today rather than those living at the time the movement began.

Our past gets in the way because we don't look far enough back. We stop at the point in the past that justifies what we do rather than going beyond that to the root to discover what we should be doing. Being radical means literally what it says, looking back beyond all of these and discovering what is at the root. Great movements, denominations, our church, all began because people in their time were committed to radical faith. They saw the need to do things differently, to do things 'in order to' rather than just 'because'.

As a result of their radical faith, new structures, new ways of communicating, new ways of being community, new ways of worshipping together came into being. But what to them was 'different', over succeeding generations has become our custom. They responded to their time, their moment, and did what needed to be done then. It was right for their time but we must not be constrained by the methods they put into place. We must go back beyond these to the root, to the message of Jesus and the apostles and ask, as they did, what must we do *now* that will help the lost to hear and understand this message.

The definition of what is right and what 'must be done' is not found by referring to any moment or movement in Church history, the defining moment must be the teaching and ministry of Jesus – this is our radix. Being radical means doing what the Bible says whether 'we do that here' or not. If our way of doing things prevents us from being obedient to Jesus' way of doing things, then we must change! This is the difference between Continuous and Discontinuous Change. This is what it means to be radical!

Discipleship

I use the word discipleship in the way that Handy uses the word change. This may be a little surprising so let me explain.

It is imperative to gain a firm grasp of what we mean when we talk of change. Change is such a difficult word to tie down, it can mean so many things. It can be positive or negative, trivial or life-changing. As Handy says:

> Change has, of course, always been what we choose to make it, good or bad, trivial or crucial … Where the same word is used to describe the trivial (a change of clothes) and the profound (a change of life), how can we easily distinguish whether it is heralding something important or not? When the same word can mean 'progress' and 'inconsistency' how should we know which is which?[3]

Change is a difficult and often unhelpful word. It can be threatening because it suggests that things are not going to be the same in the future, but doesn't provide any pointers as to whether things will be better or worse, just different.

So why use the word discipleship instead of change? The reason I do this is because I think that effective change is brought about as a result of a process of learning to do things differently. Discipleship entails learning from Jesus and it is as we learn from Him that we will bring about change that is not a desperate attempt to salvage a lost cause, or something that just makes us feel that perhaps things aren't so bad after all. Learning from Jesus will lead literally to a radical approach to how we do things and this will result in change.

Hence change is not a knee-jerk reaction, it is a process and, like any process, it is helpful to have a framework within which to keep the process moving, otherwise before long it will just get stuck. Something will be tried, it won't work and that's the end. Or something will be tried, work and then instead of being a stepping stone to something else, gradually its effectiveness will wane.

The Wheel of Learning

For change to bring about positive results it must be an ongoing process that is driven by a desire to be effective rather than merely to change things for their own sake. To provide a framework for this process I have adapted what Handy calls 'The Wheel of Learning'.

This process of effective change involves three key stages that keep the wheel of learning turning.

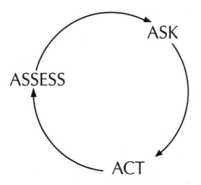

1. Ask

As mentioned earlier, if we always do what we've always done we'll always get what we've always got. I think that most of us know this is true and feel deep within that we want to do things differently, but somehow we just carry on doing pretty much the same as we've always done with pretty much the same result. I find this quote by Arthur Koestler to be so relevant to our situation: 'Habit is the denial of creativity and the negation of freedom; a self-imposed straitjacket of which the wearer is unaware.'

The only way to break out of the habit of doing things the way we have always done them is to begin to ask why we are doing them rather than just carry on. The wheel of learning is set into motion by those who ask questions, who are not satisfied with what is and ask why we do what we do and why we cannot do something else instead.

Many, many Christians are asking these questions privately. Rather than individual Christians longing to ask these questions, or small groups of disgruntled Christians asking them 'in private', now is the time to do it openly. Within every church we must provide contexts for people to raise and discuss these questions without which this process will never begin.

Jostein Gaarde wrote in his bestselling book, *Sophie's World*, 'An answer is always the stretch of the road that's behind you, only a question can point the way forward.'

So much of what happens in church is packaged and delivered. There is almost no opportunity in public meetings for any questions to be raised; this has to stop if our church will begin to make the radical changes that are necessary. But there are many things that prevent the wheel of learning being pushed into action, many reasons that questions are not asked.

Reasons we don't ask questions

Not the done thing

Many Christians and churches are afraid to take this first step because they feel that church is not a place to ask questions but rather to 'believe what they are told'. Questions are viewed as a challenge to authority, often with the result that they are not considered in an open healthy environment. Instead they become the basis for dissatisfaction that may result in several little groups of discontented people who each feel that 'they' (the others) haven't quite got it right. With increasing frequency now the result is that people just give up on church and continue with their faith without the hassle of it. 'What's the point of going there, nobody listens to me!' is a sentence I have heard more and more in recent years.

Ignorance is bliss

Alternatively, we don't question things because we find safety and a huge amount of comfort in the familiar. It is not what we are changing to that scares us, it is that we find safety in what we have. This safety in familiarity means that we see change as a threat rather than necessary change that we know must take place.

The result of this is that we believe that we could not achieve what needs to be done anyway. 'What is the point of giving up what we are familiar with if the new stuff isn't going to work any better?' In which case we've lost what we value and gained nothing in return.

We can, therefore, view the opportunity before us as too big, too hard, beyond our resources … Any new suggestion can be greeted with 'why?' which usually means 'what's the point?' It is time for a new question – 'why not?'

The challenge of familiarity

Many of us find it almost impossible to accept the statement that there is nothing that we do that has to be done the way we do it. Many of us believe it to be true, but the difficulty comes when the truth of it is applied to our situation. We have become so used to doing things the way we do them that we cannot imagine doing them differently.

The challenge of choice

At the other end of the scale is the challenge of choice. Because there is no blueprint, we could, if we are prepared to do things differently, choose to do any number of different things. This can be hard because we don't know which to do.

A combination of the above leaves many of us in a position where we know that something has to be done, but we wait for somebody else to do it just in case we shouldn't really or in case it goes wrong.

But if things are to change then questions must begin to be asked. We must begin to consider in our churches, 'If this is true then what should we do?'

There are obviously so many questions that could be asked. And there are numerous helpful initiatives that have emerged that can help churches to raise these questions in far more detail than I can do here. I do suggest though that every church, at least for one Sunday, or perhaps for a month – a special 'month of Sundays' – stops doing what it always does and considers one or both of these key questions.

1. Our church runs a variety of activities. To what extent do each of these reveal, conceal or corrupt the message of Jesus, that He came to seek and to save what was lost?

2. If Jesus had just appeared to us, following His resurrection, and sent us to be witnesses, what would we do to fulfil this commission? (In answering this question remember that we have just been sent so we are not bound by any of the things that the church currently does because it does not yet exist!)

Asking these questions openly and honestly will, I am sure, lead to the desire for things to be done differently and more effectively, but asking the questions is only the beginning. The next step is to do something – to act.

2. Act

Asking the right questions is crucial to setting the wheel of learning into motion but the answer to the questions is to be found in doing things not merely talking about them. This is where the wheel can easily get stuck, but it mustn't.

We so often crush the possibility of doing something effective because we only know the familiar. Jim Goodwin said, 'The impossible is often the untried.'

How right he is; how easy it would be for a church to raise questions and conclude that there is nothing that can be done about it. This hasty admission of defeat is not wisdom but fear, fear of what has not been done before. And Jean-Louis Etienne adds a dimension to this thought that is so appropriate, 'Everything looks impossible for the people who never try anything.' It is only once a church begins to do things that what seemed impossible begins to be seen as within reach.

Perhaps the best summary of these two quotes is another that I came across. 'If you really want to do something you'll find a way; if you don't you'll find an excuse.' We haven't got any more time for excuses; something needs to be done and it needs to be done now.

There are two aspects to the action stage. They are two parts of the same thing and must happen alongside each other.

Teaching

This part of the process involves looking into the Bible for some answers to the questions that are now being raised.

Many churches value teaching and rightly see it as a key part of their ministry. However, in many instances, the method of teaching is the same as the method introduced hundreds of years ago. Teaching is often synonymous with preaching and much of what is taught is to the whole congregation together at one time. It is done in this way 'because' that is how we do it rather than 'in order to' be effective in helping Christians to become effective disciples.

There are a number of reasons why effective teaching requires more than a monologue delivered on a Sunday:

• The time allowed for the teaching is normally set by the length of the service. It cannot be possible that every teaching topic can be properly dealt with in the same amount of time every week.
• People in the congregation are likely to be different from one another.

Trying to speak to a diverse group of people at one go inevitably leads to the message being too general.

- Most learning that takes place outside the church is now interactive as opposed to being one person addressing everybody else. We learn by discussion, by speaking as well as listening.
- Most people are used to media in communication and expect pictures as well as words. In addition, some find it difficult to concentrate for long periods.

To overcome these obstacles, churches must teach in new ways. But these new ways should not be restricted to changing the length of the sermon and using a video projector. Important as these things may be, they are not really different, they are doing the same thing in a different way.

Our teaching must allow for opportunities to 'speculate' and investigate possible answers, to suggest and to dream. Such 'learning' can never take place only in a Sunday morning congregation context. People will learn more effectively through small groups and open forums than by merely listening to a sermon.

If people do not contribute something to the formulation of the idea they do not learn anything nor do they feel a part of the process. It is always somebody else's idea that they may or may not agree with. This involves empowerment of everybody so that they understand what is being planned and the part they may have to play in the fulfilment.

Some key thoughts as to how this teaching should take place:

1. It should be interactive – seminar/workshop style teaching as well as direct teaching 'from the front'.
2. It should include opportunities for people to share in small groups.
3. It should bear in mind that people are not all at the same place in their understanding and experience.

Perhaps more important than any of the above is that teaching should never be done in a vacuum. As the Chinese proverb says: 'I hear, I forget. I see, I remember. I do, I understand.' People really learn not by what they hear but by what they do! Even more important than the style of teaching is to realise that just because we have told people something it does not mean we have taught them anything. They will learn as they do and opportunities for action must be seen as part of the teaching ministry of the church.

Doing

Doing is an intrinsic part of learning and we are, I am glad to say, beginning to take this seriously within our churches, but we must do so more. For too long teaching has covered the 'theory' but not the 'practice'. What is staggering about this is that the Bible itself is so clear on this matter.

Matthew, in his Gospel, records these words of Jesus at the end of the Sermon on the Mount:

> 'Therefore everyone who hears these words of mine and *puts them into practice* is like a wise man who built his house on the rock. The rain came down, the streams rose, and the winds blew and beat against that house; yet it did not fall, because it had its foundation on the rock. But everyone who hears these words of mine and does not put them into practice is like a foolish man who built his house on the sand. The rain came down, the streams rose, and the winds blew and beat against that house, and it fell with a great crash.' (Matt. 7:24–27, my italics)

Familiar words, but do we really get what Jesus is saying? Presumably the reason the second house fell was because it did not have its foundation on the rock. Obviously it is the stability of the rock that helps the house to stand against the elements, but what is the rock? It is this part that I think we so easily get wrong. I have often heard it referred to as 'the Word of God'. But this is clearly not the case. The rock is not the Word of God because both men hear Jesus' words! The rock is 'putting these words into practice'. It is as we do (not just listen to) what the Word says that we are transformed and can be used by God to transform others.

James, in his letter, puts it like this:

> Do not merely listen to the word, and so deceive yourselves. Do what it

says. Anyone who listens to the word but does not do what it says is like a man who looks at his face in a mirror and, after looking at himself, goes away and immediately forgets what he looks like. But the man who looks intently into the perfect law that gives freedom, and continues to do this, not forgetting what he has heard, but doing it – he will be blessed in what he does.' (James 1:22–25)

James, like Jesus, is very strong in his language; he points out that people who just listen to teaching from the Word and then do nothing with it are deceiving themselves. They are deceiving themselves because they mistakenly think that God wants us to know His Word as an end in itself. He doesn't, He wants us to know it in order that we will do it!

So, doing is part of the learning process; hence if Christians are to learn they must be given opportunities to do. Listening is only a small part of the learning process, yet sadly in many churches it is the only type of learning that is available.

3. Assess

There is another key step in the learning process without which once again the wheel gets stuck. This is not an add-on step, it is every bit as crucial as the others but perhaps the most neglected of all within the Church. Many churches have tried something and if it has not worked they have just stopped doing it 'never to be tried again'. If it has worked it has normally continued while, and long after, it still works.

The reason for this, and the reason that many churches do not continue to develop through this process is that they do not assess or evaluate what has happened and learn from it.

There is perhaps a key reason for this that cannot be ignored if we are to keep the wheel moving. Many Christians have a huge fear of failure and of making mistakes. We are so afraid of looking silly that we would prefer not to hear what we have done well and what perhaps could have been done better. However nobody improves without this kind of help and it is sad that church, of all places, is where people find it most difficult to fail.

Difficult as this step is, it must be worked through and, as this happens, it will lead to a new understanding of fellowship and mission.

Key to this step is providing an atmosphere in which people feel it is safe to make mistakes. This is crucial because making mistakes is an essential part of the learning process; in just about every area of life we learn more as a result of the things we get wrong than the things we get right. This is no less true when it comes to the Christian life.

Effective churches must be communities where people are able to make mistakes and where they can then be helped to improve.

Again, Charles Handy is helpful on this subject: 'A learning organisation will try to turn mistakes into learning opportunities, not by using them as sticks to beat with but as case-studies for discussion.' [4]

Summary

It is within the grasp of every Christian community, and every Christian, to be an agent for transformation in the world. The message of Jesus can be revealed through us as His people. The final two chapters explore how first communities and then individuals can be effective witnesses to the message of Jesus.

It is a time for new imaginings, of windows opening even if some doors close. We need not stumble backwards into the future, casting long glances at what used to be; we can turn round and face a changed reality. It is, after all, a safer posture if we want to keep on moving. [5]

9

Witnessing communities

I was speaking at a town-wide event in Oxfordshire as part of a launch weekend for an initiative called Sound Nation. Many people from the local churches took part in leading different aspects of the service. For me, the most memorable was a priest who led the prayers. He had written the prayer down in advance and as he read it aloud I felt as if I had just prayed one of the most meaningful and relevant prayers of my life. It went something like this:

> *Father help us to knock down the walls that divide us and use the bricks from the rubble to build bridges into our community.*

What a prayer, and if God were to answer it what a difference it would make to every church. Churches working together with one aim, to be bridges that people can cross in order to discover the truth about Jesus. What is exciting in these days is that God is answering this prayer. There are countless examples in numerous towns and cities, where churches are working together on exciting and innovative projects, where it is Jesus, not any particular denomination or church, that is the important thing. It is this approach of working together to communicate the message of Jesus that must become the normal way that Christians go about things because, as exciting as these things are, there is still a way to go.

Christian communities can and will become witnessing communities as they begin to consider a basic but crucial question: why do we meet together?

Meeting together

Christians meet together on a regular basis, most frequently to attend worship services but, in spite of these frequent meetings, only very few Christians have the confidence and desire to make Jesus known to those outside the Church. The reason for this is that we have somehow forgotten that the purpose of meeting together is 'in order to' help Christians become effective disciples and witnesses, rather than 'because' it is what Christians do.

Many Christians I meet have a growing feeling that what we do when we meet together is not quite working. While this feeling continues to grow, many churches still continue to do substantially the same as they have always done. It is as if there are things that we must not tamper with because they must be done in a certain way. I think there lingers in many of us this feeling that somehow thinking this way can prevent us from asking important questions about our meetings. If attending a service, in and of itself earns salvation, then all the believer has to do is turn up and do what is required, and little thought has to be given to what happens at the meeting. But if our meeting together is in order to help Christians to become more effective then a great deal of attention should be given to what we do.

If our churches are to reform, to become communities that witness, I think it is vital that the following statement becomes our starting point.

> There is no biblical justification for any belief that attending church services on a Sunday, in and of itself, makes any difference whatsoever to a person's eternal destiny.

If we are to be radical, we need to go back beyond the inherited view that attending church is somehow in and of itself an act that God will reward. We need to consider why early Christians met together.

It seems clear that their meeting together was never meant to be something that earned the reward of God's favour. It was intended to be a means by which Christians could be built up and encouraged in the faith so that they could make a positive difference for Jesus in their everyday lives.

Hebrews 10:25 is a verse that is often used as a basis for Christians attending worship on a regular basis: 'Let us not give up meeting together, as some are in the habit of doing, but let us encourage one another – and all the more as you see the Day approaching.'

This verse does not contain a hint of any notion that faithful attendance at the meeting will please God and earn a reward. The purpose is 'mutual encouragement'. The previous verse underlines this: 'And let us consider how we may spur one another on towards love and good deeds' (Heb. 10:24).

The writer to the Hebrews was addressing a difficult situation. Many of the Hebrew/Jewish followers of Jesus were tempted to turn back from following Him and revert to Judaism. It is perfectly understandable. Followers of Jesus were being persecuted for their faith whereas Judaism was a religion that was not persecuted. It is for this reason that the writer underlines throughout the letter that there is no turning back because Judaism is incomplete without Christ. Rather, what they must do, is move forward.

'But we are not of those who shrink back and are destroyed, but of those who believe and are saved' (10:39). It is interesting that in this verse the word 'believe' is used as the alternative to 'shrink back'. Believing faith is an active thing, as Paul had said to the Galatians, 'The only thing that counts is faith expressing itself through love' (Gal. 5:6).

So the purpose of their meeting together was that they needed one another in order to spur each other on and encourage one another to put their faith into action rather than shrink back. Their meetings had a purpose, and so must ours.

We may not face the same persecution as these early Christians, but faith has been kept behind closed doors and Christians have been shrinking back for too long. Now is the time to go out and 'express' our faith in love. It is a time of great opportunity!

If we are going to grasp this moment we need each other. It is transformed people that God can use to transform the world. The purpose of our meetings should be that those who gather will be transformed rather than expected merely to conform to a ritual.

Community not congregation

The Church in the New Testament was not formed as a congregation of individuals, it was a community, or body of people, that belonged to Christ and to one another. Those that originally accepted the message were baptised and then, Luke tells us, they:

> ... devoted themselves to the apostles' teaching and to the fellowship, to the breaking of bread and to prayer ... All the believers were together and had everything in common ... Every day they continued to meet together in the temple courts ... and ate together with glad and sincere hearts ... (Acts 2:42–47)

Something was happening, these new believers were part of a dynamic movement, they were witnessing people's lives being transformed and these transformed people were being joined to a dynamic community. This was not just true of the church in Jerusalem but, as the message of Jesus spread across the world, it resulted in the coming together of believers into new communities.

It is by being an active member of a community, not a passive member in a congregation, that Christians will become effective in witnessing. It was this being part of a community that helped these early Christians to stand against the opposition that they faced. It is church as community not congregation that provides the background in which the New Testament was written. It becomes hard to apply some of the teaching of Paul and others, written to churches that were communities, to churches today that have little community feel and are merely congregations.

So it seems clear that the Church in the New Testament was not a place where individuals went to earn salvation. It was a community to which each person belonged. So strong was the sense of community that it was likened to a body in which each part was valuable, significant and necessary for the body to be fully effective. It is this sense of community that must be rediscovered; without it individual Christians will attend church out of a sense of duty and feel totally isolated and unsupported in their daily witness. The result will be that most Christians will therefore not witness.

I was speaking at a conference on 'Being a witness in the work place'. I delivered what I hoped had been a helpful seminar on some ideas of how to reach out to others at work. At the end, a man came up to me, politely thanked me and then said, 'I'm not sure about reaching other men at work, it's the most I can do to hold on to my own faith.' His church, I discovered as we spoke, provided him with no support, teaching or encouragement whatsoever to help him survive, let alone make an impact, in his working environment. No wonder he struggled, he was left to do it all on his own!

Speaking at church after church I discover this scenario repeated over and over again. There is often little or no mutual support for people to encourage and equip them to be effective in sharing their faith. One church I was working with recently did say that they had run an evangelism training session a couple of years ago so people ought to know how to share their faith. But Christians need more than a training session every couple of years if they are going to be effective. They need to be helped continually. The life of the church must focus on helping Christians to be effective, rather than pouring most of its energy into running services that are only a small part of what Christians need.

Many churches now are replacing some Sunday sermons with seminars, led by different people. These seminars contain specific teaching to a specific group. This is part, but not all, of the answer. There is a need also for small groups of Christians to meet and pray for one another as they seek to share their faith. This provides support and accountability and the context for specific and honest prayer.

It is at this point that the difficulty of the challenge of choice becomes evident. There are so many things that could be done, that nothing happens. There have been numerous books and words written outlining models of church and ways of doing church effectively. I do not want to suggest a format for how it should be done, instead I want to suggest that there are some needs that each Christian has that should be taken seriously by every local church. It is these needs that should be met in the times that the Christians meet together. What each church actually does should be something that in many ways is unique to that group of people because each group will be slightly different.

The key ingredients

There are, I would suggest, four things that all Christians need if they are to be an effective part of a witnessing community. If we are to witness for Jesus in our daily lives, we need to be: educated, enthused, encouraged and equipped.

Educated

Teaching is vital if Christians are to understand and grasp the message of Jesus. The teaching ministry of the church must take into account the fact that we are not all in the same place with regards to our spiritual maturity and understanding.

Enthused

Enthused literally means to be 'filled with God', and this being filled with God is vital if Christians are to become effective witnesses. We will never muster up the desire to share our faith with others on our own. It is Christ in us that gives us the passion and desire to share Him with others. Each of us needs to have opportunities to remember and experience the reality of Christ living in us. A witnessing community must provide regular opportunities for those who gather to be enthused, or filled with God.

Encouraged

Encouraged literally means to be filled with courage. The majority of Christians are not naturally brave and this lack of bravery is due in part to fear but also is largely due to the fact that we can so often feel isolated.

Witnessing is often difficult and disappointing, it can result in opposition, or it can sometimes seem to have no result, as a Christian seeks to witness but nobody seems to be interested. If we are to continue in our witness rather than give up because it is just too difficult, then it is not an option but vital that Christians regularly and constantly encourage one another.

Equipped

Christians who are enthused by God and encouraged by those around them are far more likely to want to witness. Their witness will be helped immensely if they are properly equipped.

The model of church that many have inherited is one that seeks to achieve all these vital needs in a worship service. Being radical allows us to start from a different place. Rather than ask, 'How do we achieve these vital needs in one service?', it allows us to say, 'What kind of "meetings together" do we need to put in place to achieve these things?' Starting with a blank timetable and filling it in with meetings at a time most convenient for those who will benefit will be far more effective than trying to achieve everything within constraints that we have inherited.

There are a number of ways that Christians can meet together that can each play their part in helping these four vital needs to be met most effectively.

Celebration and worship

There is an important place for large gatherings where Christians can worship God in exciting and deeply meaningful ways. Music and singing in worship can be so powerful in helping Christians to remember and appreciate how good the good news is. Anointed preaching can encourage, inspire and challenge us to move on with God, to witness for Him. Many churches may find it difficult to run events of this nature but this should not be a cause for despair because there are things that every church can do.

One thing is to look around at the variety of helpful conferences and festivals that take place. Many churches have been, and continue to be, helped by going as a group to such events. In addition, in many towns and cities now, there is an emergence of churches coming together for praise and worship events, sometimes 'in the park', often in church buildings. Developing these further and seeing them as key events to enthuse and encourage Christians could be so helpful as the Christian community in an area benefits from doing things together.

As well as looking outside to other things, each local church could make their worshipping together so much more meaningful. If the question is asked, 'What will help us to meet with and be transformed by God?' rather than 'Which hymns or songs shall we sing this week and what will the sermon be on?' the change could be immense. Each Christian could contribute different things according to his or her experience and gifts. The meeting could involve food, music, visual media, sharing of what God is doing. There is much technology available to everybody now. We can use CD players and DVDs – most people have got them at home! We could also be creative and try things out; we could experiment with drama, with music, with poetry, with anything that is an expression of the gifts of those that contribute. This approach to meeting together is possible for all churches regardless of how small or large.

Our meeting need not be the same next time as it was last time. The great tragedy is that we have become so familiar with an inherited way of doing church that we feel we have to do certain things in a certain way. We continue to do things in this way even if nobody within the church has the gifts to do them, and nobody is being helped by what we do.

As a student training for the ministry, I once went to preach at a small church in the south of England. I remember receiving a phone call from the church secretary a few days before. He asked me, with a degree of panic in his voice, if I could play the piano or guitar. I said that unfortunately I couldn't. He then said that they were really stuck because their regular pianist was ill and their reserve pianist was on holiday, what were they going to do? I suggested that perhaps it might be OK if we didn't sing, perhaps we could have an informal gathering instead.

When I arrived on the Sunday morning I have to say I was not surprised to discover that they had found a pianist. It was not her fault that she didn't know any of the songs that had been chosen, because she was in her prime as a pianist many years before most of the songs were written. As we worked our way through the hymns, slowly and painfully, I thought, not for the first time, and not for the last, 'Why do we do things in church just because they are what makes us feel like we are being a church?'

I cannot be the only person who has been at church, in the middle of a hymn that was written to help those who sang it to be 'enthused', wondering why on earth we are doing this, because the pianist can't play it.

The great thing about being truly radical is that it is liberating. There is nothing stopping us making our meetings together valuable and beneficial if we ask, 'What will help us?' rather than 'Who is playing the music and who is preaching this week?' If we plan meetings 'in order to' rather than 'because'.

Smaller groups

But meeting together doesn't mean that everybody has to meet together all the time. Christians will be helped by meeting in a variety of other smaller groups. Again, these groups will be most effective if they are set up in answer to the question 'what will be helpful?' rather than 'how do we get people to come?'

There are many churches benefiting from this approach, and once again it provides a great opportunity to be creative. These smaller groups can be all sorts of things, some more obviously spiritual, like cells, house groups, young mums' Bible study groups, prayer groups. Others may seem less obviously spiritual, such as men's football teams or breakfast meetings – sport and food seem to be quite helpful things for getting people together. Some of these meetings together can be organised by the church leaders but many will be at the initiative of like-minded people in the church who share common interests and want to meet together. It is often in these smaller informal groups that much encouragement takes place.

Pairs

As well as these smaller 'meetings together' there is an opportunity for enthusing and encouraging that seems to happen far too seldom. I have always been interested in the fact that Jesus sent His disciples out in pairs. A type of 'meeting together' that would help many Christians to witness effectively, would be for each to have one other person to talk with, pray with and possibly meet with on a regular basis. Two people can be much more honest with each other than it is possible to be in a larger group. They can be specific and real about their victories and their failures. They can affirm, encourage, comfort and challenge one another.

Equipping opportunities

In addition to regular planned or unplanned informal meetings that take place within the community life of the church there is also a need for regular equipping of Christians. Some of this can take place as part of the teaching and small group meetings that are already taking place. But, in addition, there is a constant need for Christians in a witnessing community to be equipped. The content of any sessions for equipping will be driven both by the skills required to accomplish what is planned, and the particular needs of those who attend.

There are two dimensions to effective equipping.

1. *Skills training.* This is the more obvious dimension and needs to be delivered by either those within or from outside your church who have the necessary skills.

2. *Gaining confidence.* Perhaps less obvious but just as important, is that Christians gain confidence. It is the lack of confidence that is the biggest problem for most. Equipping is not merely telling people how to do things and then leaving them to get on with it.

It is important to remember that effective equipping must go beyond the theory. As the wheel of learning demonstrated previously (see p.117), people will learn most when they act, put what they are learning into practice, and then assess, review what they have done and learn from what they did well and any mistakes they may have made.

Making it work

Viewing church as a community in which every person has a contribution, has implications for all in the community. Each person has a ministry, but this does not mean that chaos should reign. While meeting together is 'in order to', this does not mean that individuals just do their own thing. There is an even greater need for leadership in a witnessing community. The fundamental difference is that the role of leaders changes, they now lead others into ministry as opposed to doing it all themselves.

Role of leaders

In the New Testament, during the phase of 'Transform' (see pp.92–93), churches were clearly communities where each person had an active role:

> … so in Christ we who are many form one body, and each member belongs to all the others. We have different gifts, according to the grace given us. If a man's gift is prophesying, let him use it in proportion to his faith. If it is serving, let him serve; if it is teaching, let him teach; if it is encouraging, let him encourage; if it is contributing to the needs of others, let him give generously; if it is leadership, let him govern diligently; if it is showing mercy, let him do it cheerfully. (Rom. 12:5–8)

For these diverse gifts to be developed and utilised most effectively, leaders were given to prepare the others in the community for ministry:

> It was he who gave some to be apostles, some to be prophets, some to be evangelists, and some to be pastors and teachers, to prepare God's people for works of service, so that the body of Christ may be built up until we all reach unity in the faith and in the knowledge of the Son of God and become mature, attaining to the whole measure of the fulness of Christ. (Eph. 4:11–12)

Fundamental to the church becoming a witnessing community was a sense of shared ownership and vision among all those that belonged. Being radical is rediscovering this view of church. The church is people, a community, and each person within the community has a part to play.

The role of leaders must be to equip and encourage those in the community to grow and develop as believers and to help them to be effective in their local community.

Role of members

This will depend upon where those that belong to the church are at. What seems clear, as a guiding principle, is that people can only witness to what they know. Therefore if they are going to be effective in witnessing to others about Jesus then it is vital that they know Him for themselves.

It is impossible to be specific here about every church, but it has been my experience that most churches are made up of a large number of people who have been 'in the church' since they were born. They may have always felt part of the community and have been baptised or confirmed. Their membership may be the result of a conversion to Christ, so have been transformed, or it may be the result of their conforming to the church. What makes it difficult to be sure is that those who have been transformed and those who have conformed will have been through a similar initiation process.

Also in many churches there are a number of people, often but not always a smaller number, that have not grown up in the church. These people are more likely to have been transformed because they did not inherit the faith from their parents.

The challenge is how to help all of these people to move on and experience the reality of Jesus transforming them and through them transforming others.

A suggested step

A key resource produced by the organisation I work with is also called *More to Life*. (See the Appendix for more information.) This resource contains DVDs and magazines filled with stories of people from a variety of backgrounds who have come to faith in Jesus. Their stories are very different, some dramatic, some very 'normal'. Often, as part of an outreach with a church, we show the DVD to those who have come to the training session. Once they have watched it through we ask them to comment on which stories they found most interesting. Then we ask them, in twos or threes, to share their own story with one another. This 'story' includes how they came to faith but also what God is doing in their lives currently. It is always amazing to hear people saying afterwards that they knew hardly anything about how others had come to faith, or about how God is involved in their lives now. But sharing like this is a very non-threatening and encouraging way of building faith into the community.

Another suggested step

There is a growing number of courses being produced that churches can use to help those outside of church discover Jesus. Many churches have benefited from running these courses firstly with the people that already come. Going through Christian basics in this way has resulted in many church members coming to real faith in Christ, and many more understanding things about their faith that they had never felt they could ask about because they felt they ought to know.

A further suggested step

This is not so much a step as a way of going about things. Regardless of whether a church uses the more formal suggestions mentioned above, a key way of helping those within the church to be transformed is to encourage and provide either formal or informal opportunities for those within the church to talk about their faith with one another.

How do we measure it?

A great challenge for a church that moves from being a group that anticipates people will conform to it, is that it will need to measure the effectiveness of its ministry in a different way. Many churches measure themselves by how many people come to a Sunday service. A witnessing community will be measured not by how many come, but by the impact being made by those who go. How many lives are being touched and influenced and helped by those who are witnessing to Jesus? This measure, far harder to calculate but far more helpful, is the true measure of the witnessing church.

When I was pastor of a church, I remember once having a conversation with a friend who was pastoring a nearby church. He said that he could not wait for revival to come, when people would be queuing up to get into the church. I told him that I think revival will not result in people queuing up to get into church; it will result in those that know Jesus becoming committed to leaving the safety and familiarity of church to go into the world with the message of Jesus. But, of course, he was partly right, the result of Christians witnessing to those around them will be that some, or perhaps many, will become interested in Jesus. But these interested people will not be very keen to join in with a series of rituals and customs that are meaningless to them.

Witnessing communities must, at the same time, be welcoming communities.

Welcoming communities

Mother Theresa once said, 'There is more hunger for love and appreciation in this world than for bread.' Around every church there are countless numbers of people looking for acceptance and love. Tragically, for most, the last place they would look is the church. Yet surely the message of Jesus is directed at these very people! The reason that they don't come is because they have got the wrong message. People looking for love and acceptance and even for hope and security are not likely to come to a place where they anticipate that all that goes on will be strange and where they will have to go through a series of what, to them, are meaningless rituals.

Of course it is true that many churches today do things that are nothing like what those outside presume goes on. I remember a lady once saying to me, 'If only they would come they would see that it's nothing like they think, it's really good.' In one way I agree with her, but the problem is that they are not going to come along and find out. Even if they did they might not think it was that good, because 50 minutes of singing followed by 50 minutes of talking, followed by more singing, is not always that appealing to people who never sing outside of the bath.

It is great that this lady appreciated what happened in her church. But this should lead, not to wishing more people would turn up and find out how good it is, but to those experiencing it going to those who will never come, and witnessing to their faith in Jesus.

Where does the welcome begin?

Our welcome must extend beyond the boundaries of Sunday church – we need to 'welcome' people in their safety zones not ours. Many churches 'warmly welcome' visitors to their services and, quite rightly, often have people on the door who smile and welcome people as they arrive. This is good and right but should not be the extent of our welcome. The welcome of the witnessing church will extend far beyond the church doors, and the time of our services. We must take the message of Jesus into their safety zones and help them to see that God welcomes them into His kingdom.

Another of Jesus' best-known parables makes this point so well. The parable of the Good Samaritan in Luke 10:25–37, as with so many of Jesus' parables, is in answer to a question. On this occasion the question was asked by an expert in the law; he asked, 'What must I do to inherit eternal life?' (v.25). In answer to his question, Jesus referred the man to the law, in which he was an expert, and said, 'What is written in the Law? … How do you read it?' (v.26). In reply, the expert in the law quoted from Deuteronomy and Leviticus: ' "Love the Lord your God with all your heart and with all your soul and with all your strength and with all your mind"; and, "Love your neighbour as yourself" ' (v.27).

This summary of the law identifies the relationship between loving God and loving other people. Having commended his answer, Jesus said to the teacher of the law, 'Do this and you will live' (v.28).

But this is not the end of the matter. Luke records, 'But he wanted to justify himself, so he asked Jesus, "And who is my neighbour?"' (v.29).

It is in answer to this question that Jesus told the parable. The teacher of the law was asking, 'Who must I love to fulfil the requirement of the law?' The parable made it clear that he asked the wrong question.

The whole point of this parable is that it shows that those who love God should not limit their love to those they have to love to fulfil the law. Jesus made it clear that loving your neighbour involves being a neighbour to everyone, regardless of who they are. The shocking truth of the parable is that the religious people pass by the man in need and it was the sworn enemy, the Samaritan, who expressed love to the unfortunate man who had been attacked.

The challenge to the local church is that it shows that love is active. The parable goes far beyond 'Who do we have to welcome to our Sunday worship?' It powerfully demonstrates once again that 'faith expresses itself through love'. The parable says go and be a neighbour to those within the local community and extend the welcome that God loves them.

This principle of taking the welcome beyond the confines of our own safety zones will result in the new way of measuring church that was referred to a little earlier. This is because it will be much harder to define who does and who doesn't belong in the church.

There has been a great deal of discussion around the subject of 'belonging' in the church. Much of this has taken place as part of the three 'B's' of belonging, believing and behaving. This is a key debate as it addresses the very issues of what the church is aiming to achieve and how it will be effective.

The traditional order of the three 'B's', during the times when the church has been able to rely upon people merely conforming, has been.

Behave ⟶ Believe ⟶ Belong

Those who *behave* in the appropriate way: that is, attend services regularly, will reach the point where they pass through an initiation that demonstrates that they *believe*, following which they are known as proper members and now fully *belong*.

This model will not be effective in a witnessing church because those that are being witnessed to will not be prepared to behave, by conforming to our customs, before they believe and belong.

I have heard suggestions that perhaps, in a welcoming church it should be turned upside down.

Belong ⟶ Believe ⟶ Behave

It is not, though, as simple as that. There is a great deal to be gained from placing belonging at the beginning; to say that people are valued and welcome even if they have not yet reached a point where they would say that they believe and want to behave like those who attend the church. But I am not sure it is that tidy. The model is probably very messy, more like a fried egg than a poached one.

Belonging/Believing/Behaving Model

People are people and therefore do not fit easily into simple models. There will be some who belong and behave like Christians, but do not yet believe. There will be some who come to faith but do not yet behave like Christians. Because the model is messy, it will mean that many of our traditional comfort zones will disappear and we will need to explore how to be welcoming to people in a whole variety of contexts – not just at the church door.

Some key principles

Again, each church will need to work out the specifics of how they will do this for themselves. There are, however, some important guiding principles.

The importance of 'discovery opportunities'

As people will no longer conform to our way of doing things out of custom or habit, they will not come to hear the message of Jesus being preached. If we are to help people understand the message of Jesus, our church must provide a variety of opportunities for people to find out about Him. These should take place at times that need not be Sunday mornings, in places that need not be the church building and enquirers should have the opportunity to ask questions rather than merely listen to what is said.

We should not make it difficult for those coming to faith

We are in a position rather like the Early Church in Antioch. People then were coming to faith who had not previously followed Jewish customs. This is the situation in which we will find ourselves as we seek to be communities that welcome those who have not been brought up in the Church.

When Eisenhower was president of Columbia University in New York, before he became President of the USA, he received a deputation from the faculty. Could he, they asked, please use his authority to stop the students walking over the grass in the main quadrangle.

'Why do they walk on the grass?' he asked.

'Because it is the easiest way to get from the main entrance to the central hall.'

'If that's the way they are going to go,' he said, 'then cut a pathway there.' Problem solved.

Making it easy for those coming to faith must be understood correctly.

The 'difficulty' that should be avoided is the imposition of unhelpful customs on those coming to faith. It does not mean that we should make it easy by diluting the gospel, by removing the requirements that followers of Jesus seek to live holy and transformed lives. On the contrary, helping all those who have faith and those coming to faith, to live transformed lives, is key to both the witnessing and welcoming aspects of the church.

We must help them to live transformed lives

God's purpose in sending Jesus was that those who followed Him would live transformed lives. The welcoming church must be a community that helps those who come to faith to become disciples of Jesus.

As new people come to faith in Jesus they will present a challenge. They, like those currently in the church, will need to be educated, enthused, encouraged and equipped. It may be that new ways of meeting together will need to be introduced. New meetings that are arranged 'in order to' help these new believers to grow, not 'because' these are the meetings that we have.

Getting started

A month of Sundays

This is just a thought, a way to get started. No church has to do what I suggest, you could ignore it, or you could adapt it and improve it. It is included as a way of helping you think how you might take the first or the next step towards reforming and becoming a transformed and transforming, or witnessing, community.

Why not have 'a month of Sundays', where you don't just do what you've always done? Meet together at the same time, in the same place, but instead of going through the familiar service do something else instead.

Rather than have a formal service 'because' that is what always happens, have an informal gathering 'in order to' think about how you could become a witnessing community. As it is informal it would be good if there were coffee and biscuits around. It could also naturally flow into having lunch together once or twice during the month.

I suggest below a possible way that it could happen, but as I have said, each church could do it in the way that is most helpful to them.

1st Sunday – Hear from each other. Encourage people to talk about the difference that Jesus is making in their lives. This can be encouraging.

2nd Sunday – Talk to each other. Encourage people to talk about how they feel that the church could reach the community. What would they change about the church and why? What do they really value about the church?

3rd Sunday – Plan with each other. How could the church help those within to reach the people that they want to reach? What kind of church would they be happy to invite friends to?

4th Sunday – Pray with each other. This praying should be specific and honest, probably in small groups and about real things.

At the end of the month of Sundays lots of things will have emerged: ideas, challenges, frustration, vision. Having stopped what the church normally does for a month, now will be the time to start doing things that we believe will be effective, things 'in order to' not things 'because'.

10

Witnessing Christians

The Early Church impacted the world because it had a simple message that was life-changing. Those being transformed by Jesus told other people about what God had done and what God was doing in their lives. This message of a loving God who could transform sinful people was accepted by many from all over the world – it was good news. This good news was so good that it just had to be talked about.

The message of Jesus is most powerfully conveyed, not by rituals and structures, but by individual Christians who share with others what Jesus is doing in their lives.

We recorded earlier the words of Red Jacket:

Brother, we are told that you have been preaching to the white people in this place. These people are our neighbours. We are acquainted with them. We will wait a little while and see what effect your preaching has upon them. If we find it does them good, makes them honest, and less disposed to cheat Indians, we will then consider again of what you have said.[1]

Red Jacket could be the boy in the church in Somerset who asked, 'Who's the bloke on the wall?' He could represent all kinds of people of different ages and from different backgrounds, men and women. If they could see that faith in Jesus was making a difference to the people that have it they might be interested in finding out more.

It is easy to fall into the trap of thinking that the challenges presented by the world around us are so great and the need to change so complicated that it is beyond us. The truth is that it isn't, it is very much within the grasp of every one of us. We live at a time when the most effective means of reaching people outside the Church will be for each Christian to live the Christian life outside their church not only inside. Living out our faith will lead to opportunities for us to talk about the difference that Jesus is making in our lives.

People will find out who the bloke on the wall is if they 'meet Him' in the lives of people that they come into contact with in their daily lives. They will not come to church out of a sense of duty or custom, they will not hear the message from their family … they will only hear as those who know Jesus, of which there are millions, become witnesses.

As we discovered in Chapter 2, the times in which we live provide a great opportunity for the gospel. This opportunity can be realised, but not by doing things how we have always done them. In a world that will not just accept things out of custom or habit, faith in Jesus will reach millions who are searching for meaning, if it is seen as a living reality rather than a series of outdated customs and dogmatic statements. C.T. Studd once wrote:

> Some wish to live within the sound
> Of church or chapel bell
> I want to run a rescue shop
> Within a yard of hell.

I came across these words on the back cover of a book about the life of Sister Gemel. The book was called *Within a Yard of Hell,* and it tells the inspiring story of Doreen Gemel who, having read a book called *God in the Slums,* dedicated herself to the care of the outcasts of society. Intrigued by the words on the cover I flicked through the book and became very impressed with Doreen's story. She was a woman who, at the age of 32, met God in a new way and then felt something inside her, a capacity for sacrifice, a desire to serve those who suffered in the slums. She did something with that feeling which resulted in her becoming Sister Gemel and establishing a shelter and refuge for drunken women in a basement near Marble Arch.

I was especially moved by an occasion in the book where Doreen remembered Ethel, a big drunken and defiant lady with whom she had walked the streets of London so many times, and who had died. I read:

> Alone in the mortuary that day, with memories surging in to quicken her emotions, she [Doreen] had knelt down and with tears streaming down her face had softly sung:

> At the close of day 'twill be sweet to say
> I have brought some lost one home.[2]

Doreen had discovered that life had more purpose than just going to work to pay the bills and visiting the theatre and enjoying the social life. She had discovered the joy of seeking the lost.

There was nothing very special about Doreen, she was an ordinary woman, but when she allowed God to move in her heart she was never the same again. She had a passion and compassion to reach lost people.

In this time of change we, as Christians, have a great opportunity to do just that, we need to gain the passion and we need to go to the lost and let them see just how much God loves them and longs for them to get to know Him. Jesus gave His life for this reason and we have the fantastic privilege of letting people know about it. We could have the thrill of bringing some lost one home.

I have to be honest and say that for me, the Christian life becomes very dry and stale if it is just about going to church. Being in the comfort zone, where everything is predictable and I can handle it on my own, may be safe but it is pretty boring.

I find that when I am in my comfort zone it doesn't take long for my faith to shrink, to become less urgent and real. The passion dries up and I forget how urgent the gospel is. But when I am in situations where faith is all there is to count on, that's when it grows and becomes so rewarding. The amazing thing I am continually discovering about God is that, as you do those things that should, humanly speaking, lead to fear and doubt, they do in fact result in confidence and faith. This faith is not in ourselves but in Jesus.

So many Christians are missing out on the thrill of seeing their faith grow and develop, of understanding God and experiencing His power, Person and provision in deep and meaningful ways. The reason they miss it is because they want to stay in the safety zone where faith is conformity to a pattern of doing church, rather than being transformed and sent out to transform the world.

Now it is time, once again, for ordinary believers, to become witnesses. In our time, when most people have little or no interest in the Church, it is witnesses that will once again transform the world. These witnesses will not all be trained theologians; they will be ordinary people with an extraordinary story. Extraordinary does not necessarily mean dramatic. It is extraordinary because it is about the difference God is making in everyday life. Jesus will reach this generation as Christians tell others about this difference that faith in Jesus makes.

Not me

So many Christians, when it comes to the thought of talking to others about Jesus, instinctively think that they would not be able to do it. We think that it is beyond us and that only brave heroic Christians can share their faith with others. This is just not the case, for two reasons.

1. The heroes were not heroes

It is so easy to presume that the early Christians, through whom Jesus transformed the world, must have been great heroes. When you read, for example, Peter saying, 'For we cannot help speaking about what we have seen and heard' (Acts 4:20), you may, like me, think: What a passion for Jesus! Especially when you bear in mind that he and John were under threat of death if they carried on witnessing.

It is always infectious to be with a person who is so excited about something that they just can't help but talk about it. Most of us have had times with people who show us photographs of their new grandson, of their holiday … and they just can't stop talking about it, 'it has changed their lives', 'it was such a great experience'. Peter just couldn't stop talking about Jesus. He was not a trained and qualified evangelist, but his life had been changed and with that came such a passion and conviction that even the threat of death could not prevent him from talking about Jesus.

So, witnessing is only for heroes, we can conclude, those who can stare death in the face and not be afraid. But Peter wasn't always such a hero! Not too long before this incident he was present when Jesus was sentenced to be crucified. In Luke 22:54ff we see a very different Peter to the one in Acts 4. Rather than not being able to help speaking about Jesus, he does the opposite – he pretends that he doesn't even know who Jesus is. He won't speak about Him at all! I have to admit that I have met more Christians who reflect this side of Peter's character than the brave and courageous one.

Luke records that Jesus had just been led away to the house of the high priest and Peter was following at a distance. As Peter sat down by a fire in the middle of the courtyard a servant girl 'looked closely at him and said, "This man was with him [Jesus]." But he denied it. "Woman, I don't know him," he said.' Peter then denied knowing Jesus again to someone else who saw him and then about an hour later to yet another person (Luke 22:54–62).

The result of this series of denials was that Peter 'went outside and wept bitterly'. Weeping bitterly is a lonely and painful experience. At such times it is possible to feel that nothing good will ever happen again, and this may have been how Peter felt. It may be how you have felt, or how you feel: 'God could never use me because I have let Him down.' If you do feel that, let me say to you that it is absolute rubbish and nothing could be further from the truth. God wants to use you even though you let Him down!

Peter, the hero who was not afraid of death, the great and fearless witness, is also Peter who was too scared to witness to those who could not harm him. Peter is like most Christians, left to themselves they can't do it; but he then learned that although he couldn't God can. That's what made the difference, not just to Peter but to all of the apostles who, John tells us in his Gospel, were together, with the doors 'locked for fear of the Jews' (20:19), and then in Acts bravely witnessing to all that Jesus had done.

Peter was not always a great witness; like most of us he was prevented by his fear. The early disciples were locked away because of their fear. For most of us it is fear that prevents us from witnessing. Maybe not fear of death but perhaps more than anything, fear of looking silly if we find ourselves in a situation where we don't know what to say in answer to questions we may be asked. It is the fear of what might happen that prevents many Christians from being witnesses.

Another incident in the life of Peter exposes a key point concerning fear. We read in Matthew 14:22–33 that the disciples were afraid when they saw Jesus walking towards them on the water, they thought He was a ghost. After Jesus had comforted them, Peter boldly stated, 'Lord, if it's you … tell me to come to you on the water' (v.28). Peter then stepped onto the water but soon began to be afraid when he saw the wind, and he called out, 'Lord, save me!' (v.30). It is Jesus' comment that is most interesting. He said to Peter, having caught him: 'You of little faith … why did you doubt?'

This is so interesting because Jesus makes a clear connection between fear and doubt. He didn't ask Peter why he was afraid, but why he doubted. Peter was afraid because he doubted that Jesus could do what he knew Jesus could do. He believed, but he didn't *believe*. Rather like the man in Mark 9 who came to Jesus and asked Him to take pity on him and his son who had an evil spirit. Their brief conversation is interesting.

The father asked, '… if you can do anything, take pity on us and help us' (v.22). To which Jesus replied, ' "If you can?" … "Everything is possible for him who believes"' (v.23).

The exclamation of the boy's father is similar to Peter's experience in the boat, and to that of so many Christians living today, who know they should be witnesses but are afraid. 'I do believe; help me overcome my unbelief!' (v.24).

The change that must take place in so many of us as Christians, if we are to grasp the opportunities that are before us, is that we must trust that Jesus can turn fear into faith.

But even as you read this you may still be thinking, 'How do I get the courage or faith?' and 'How do I get the passion in the first place?'

2. It is as you go that you know
The answer is not to wait but to start. Paul had talked of faith expressing itself through love, and it is this active faith that is real faith.

During my time as an evangelist I have visited many schools and taken assemblies as part of special outreaches. At the end of each assembly I would always invite the young people to come to the event that was held at the end of the week. Knowing that many of them would assume that a Christian event would be rubbish, I made a point of telling them how good it would be. I would then challenge them to come along and see if it was really possible to have fun and find out about God at the same time. My closing sentence was always the same, 'And remember, if you don't go you'll never know.'

In a different way this is also true of us. We will develop a passion and courage for witnessing by doing it. God wants to use you to witness to others and if you start doing it He will use you – we don't get the power before we go – we 'grow as we go'.

Jesus said, 'Go into all the world ... and I will be with you.' It is as we trust God and do it that our fears turn into faith, that our indifference to the lost is replaced by a glowing passion.

Nelson Mandela is known across the world as a man of courage and passion. But there was a time when he was not involved in the battle for the rights and liberties of those suffering under apartheid. However, he did not wake up one day and suddenly have all the passion and courage that would help him to achieve all that he did. He says, in *Long Walk to Freedom*,

> I had no epiphany, no singular revelation, no moment of truth, but a steady accumulation of a thousand slights, a thousand indignities and a thousand unremembered moments produced in me an anger, a rebelliousness, a desire to fight the system that imprisoned my people. There was no particular day on which I said, Henceforth I will devote myself to the liberation of my people; instead, I simply found myself doing so, and could not do otherwise.[3]

Many of us as Christians wait for a moment when we might be 'called' to do something about telling others about Jesus. But it is as we find ourselves doing so that the 'calling' grows.

I will always remember a young lad called Matthew who came on an evangelism training summer project that I was running. When he arrived he made it clear that he was not very good at evangelism so I was thrilled when, one evening, at the non-alcoholic cocktail bar that had been set up as an outreach, he ran up to me with a smile on his face as wide as I have ever seen. 'I don't believe it,' he said, 'he became a Christian!' Matthew had been used by God to lead somebody to Jesus and he was thrilled.

It is as we go that we know because, it is when we put our faith into practice that it works. It begins by saying to God, *OK, I know that up until now I have never really talked to other people about Jesus, I have left it to everybody else. Lord, You know every excuse I have made, every fear and doubt I have, but I want people to know what I have found so I am trusting You to help me as I tell them.*

We know as we go because we don't go alone

So it is as we go that we will know God with us. This is exactly what Jesus said would be the case for all who bear witness to Him. He promised to be with us:

'All authority in heaven and on earth has been given to me. Therefore go and make disciples of all nations, baptising them in the name of the Father and of the Son and of the Holy Spirit, and teaching them to obey everything I have commanded you. And surely I am with you always, to the very end of the age.' (Matt. 28:18–20)

John, in his Gospel, records in depth many of the last things that Jesus told His disciples before He went to die. Central to all that He said was that even though He would be going away, the disciples would not be left alone, He would continue to be with them because He would send the Holy Spirit.

'… you know him, for he lives with you and will be in you. I will not leave you as orphans; I will come to you.' (John 14:17–18)
'He will bring glory to me by taking from what is mine and making it known to you.' (John 16:14)

The Holy Spirit and witness

The key role of the Holy Spirit as being 'Christ in us' is seen later in John's Gospel. Following His resurrection, Jesus appeared to the disciples and said: ' "Peace be with you! As the Father has sent me, I am sending you." And with that he breathed on them and said, "Receive the Holy Spirit …"' (20:21–22).

Luke records: 'You are witnesses of these things. I am going to send you what my Father has promised' (24:48–49), and then a little later, 'But you will receive power when the Holy Spirit comes on you; and you will be my witnesses in Jerusalem, and in all Judea and Samaria, and to the ends of the earth' (Acts 1:8).

Jesus promised to be with His followers in the Person of the Holy Spirit. As they went, they would know this power with them, as it would be as if Jesus Himself were with them.

I remember once visiting a Christian bookshop which as well as selling books sold a number of gift items, one of which was a poster. It was of a beautiful, peaceful scene with brightly coloured flowers in the foreground. Printed on it were these words of Jesus: 'And, lo, I am with you alway, even unto the end of the world' (Matt. 28:20, KJV).

If ever a poster missed the point this must have been it. Jesus did not promise His presence so that we would enjoy the scenery, but so that we would know His presence and power in the midst of witnessing to who He is and the good news He came to communicate.

As we become witnesses there will be obstacles, but it is as we face these and experience the presence and power of God helping us, that our own faith becomes stronger. It ceases to be a faith in what God can do through others and becomes an experience of what God is doing through us.

As we begin to be good news, living and sharing the message of Jesus in our community, then so much else of what the Bible talks about ceases to be simply our doctrine, it comes alive and becomes real in our experience. Reaching the lost is not only good news for them, it is good news for us as well!

So how do I witness effectively?

The question is 'How do I start?' The answer is START!

The moment in which we live requires that evangelism is not the task of professionals but of every Christian. People will not come to church and listen to a sermon as they would previously. In a society where people are not going to come to us we must go to them.

Perhaps the most important place to start is by remembering that Jesus commanded us to be witnesses. In a court of law it is the job of the witness just to tell the truth. It is the job of the lawyer to 'prove or defend' the case and to obtain the verdict. One thing that prevents many Christians from being witnesses is that we think that a witness has to be a lawyer; we think that we need to be professional evangelists who can answer every question and 'prove, or defend, the Christian faith'. The truth is that we do not have to be 'professionals' – we have to be witnesses.

So we should not be daunted by the prospect of having to 'prove' that Christianity is true. Our witness will be effective, not because we know all the answers, but because people will see something in our lives that will arouse interest in what we believe. We don't have to know all the answers, we don't need to have read the Bible from cover to cover three times in the last year. We don't have to have been through the latest evangelism training course last week. We just need to live out our Christian lives in public and then be prepared to talk about what it is that makes us live differently.

But I have a feeling that as you are reading this you might be thinking that this may be true for other people but it's not true for you. You may well be thinking that God could never use you in this way. But He can and He will.

Why your story will reach others

As you read this heading I can almost hear you thinking, 'There's nothing very interesting about me, nothing in my story that would reach anyone'; and perhaps the thought of 'telling your story' to other people is daunting. There are a few reasons why you might feel this way but, as you will see, you have a lot to share and nothing to fear. Below are some frequent responses to the thought of telling our story to others.

'I'm not standing up in front of everyone at church!'
One of the things about going to church regularly is that over a period of time we get used to certain phrases and associate them with a certain way of doing things. This is true of the phrase 'telling your story' – it is often called our 'testimony' and this is associated with standing at the front of church and speaking to a crowd of people.

This is not what 'telling your story' is all about. The situations in which you can talk about your faith are as diverse as the situations you find yourself in. It is outside the church, one-to-one over a cup of coffee, at the hairdressers, at work, at school … that your story can be shared. It is not a presentation, or a performance, but natural conversation.

'I can't remember a moment when I became a Christian.'
I have met so many Christians who say this. They have somehow become convinced that they don't have a story to tell because they came to know Jesus gradually rather than at a 'crisis' moment. But this exposes a key mistake that many of us make when we think of our story – we think that telling our story means telling people how we came to faith in Christ. The truth is that most people won't be interested in that part of your story unless they are interested in what your faith means to you in your daily life. The story you have to tell is about 'God's involvement in your life now'. It is a story of a God who loves you and is an important part of your life.

Explaining how you came to faith may be the last thing you tell a person, after they have become interested in the living faith that you have.

'Nobody would be interested in my story. It's not dramatic enough.'
Another comment I have heard more times than I can remember. You may think you've got nothing to say to anybody because you haven't got a great and dramatic story. There is an assumption that people will only listen to you if your story is about having been on drugs, or of a miraculous healing, or that you were a convicted murderer …

The truth is that while these stories have their place, most people are fairly 'ordinary' and can be reached more effectively by stories of people who have discovered their need of God without having been 'the worst of sinners'.

The people that you will talk to are likely to live in the same area as you, probably use the same shops and schools. They live very similar lives to you except that they do not have a relationship with Jesus. Your life experience is therefore more relevant to them than a spectacular story of somebody they have never met, overcoming a situation they have never faced.

The thing that people will find most interesting is how your faith helps you in your daily life. It is these 'normal' things that are a key part of your story, that will be relevant to others facing similar challenges in their daily lives. People will be interested to know how your faith helps you as a parent, with relationships, to cope with the stresses and anxieties of life. They may also be interested to hear about ways that you believe God is involved in decisions you make, and even in answers to prayer. Your life is more interesting than you think. Things that you take for granted are totally outside the experience of many people with whom you have contact.

'People might persecute me.'
They might! Some will be interested and want to find out more, some will not be interested and not want to know. Some will see this as an opportunity to make you the brunt of their jokes, get some laughs at your expense, try to catch you out and make you 'fall'. It can be tough but that's when God with us becomes far more of a reality – we don't need Him with us in the same way when we are hiding. Also sometimes the people that seem most opposed are in fact the most interested.

'I'll probably say something wrong or really stupid.'
Speaking over many years, with many Christians, in many different parts of the world, I have concluded that it is the fear of looking stupid that is the greatest obstacle to most Christians sharing their faith. We are so afraid of saying the wrong thing, or something that sounds silly, that we decide to say nothing. But we should be encouraged and see that God doesn't require us to get everything exactly right before He uses us. I am so grateful that the same Holy Spirit who is at work in me, is at work on the person I am

sharing with, as John records: 'When he [the Holy Spirit] comes, he will convict the world of guilt in regard to sin and righteousness and judgment' (John 16:8).

And as Paul said to the Corinthian church: 'My message and my preaching were not with wise and persuasive words, but with a demonstration of the Spirit's power ...' (1 Cor. 2:4).

Paul made this point to underline the fact that it is Jesus and not men that people should follow. What he says also demonstrates, as does the teaching of Jesus in John's Gospel, that it is not our 'performance' that makes the difference, rather it is our preparedness to witness that opens up the possibility for the Holy Spirit to work.

It is not our 'stupidity' that will prevent people from hearing the message – it is our silence.

'I'm not perfect, if I tell people the truth about my life it would not be a good witness.'
You don't have to be perfect to be used; often it is when people see that we are not the finished article that they can identify with us better. They see that faith in Jesus is making a difference to our lives. Many people outside the Church think that 'religion' is only for the righteous and that doesn't include them. It is helpful for them to see the real message of Jesus being lived through us – that He accepts us with all our imperfections but is changing us. They can be accepted just as they are and Jesus can change them for the better as well.

So there are several 'reasons' that are given as to why you can't do it, but the truth is that you can. This is because people are interested in stories and your story shows that Christianity works.

People are interested in stories

Recently, we had a man in our house who was finishing off work on our new wooden floor. I made him a mug of tea and casually asked him how he was doing. I expected the usual 'fine thanks' kind of response, but not this time. He was almost in tears as he told me about his dog that had just died;

how he and his wife had had to rearrange their lives in the past few weeks to be there with the dog in the last days of his life. He told me how gutted they all were and how they miss him so much.

There, in my living room, I was suddenly experiencing a man I had never met before pouring out his heart about what was happening in his life. I was so moved. I have to confess to not being much of a dog lover, but by the time he had finished his story I was almost in tears myself.

There is possibly nothing more interesting than finding out what is going on in other people's lives. To everybody else each of us is another person, and if we talk about what is going on in our lives many people will be interested.

Is it true? vs Does it work?

Many of us think we have to be a great theologian if we are to share our faith because we imagine that faith-sharing is about convincing others that Christianity is true. We will need to convince people about creation as opposed to evolution, the historical facts about Jesus, why He is unique … The time will come when those we are trying to reach may need to ask these questions but 'Is it true?' is not the starting place for most of the people with whom you and I come into contact.

I remember speaking at an Easter event some years ago. I presented the case for Christ, I underlined the historical reliability of the events of Jesus' death and resurrection. I did a good job.

At the end of the event a lady whose Christian friend had brought her along, came up to me. I asked her what she thought of the event and she said that it had been nothing like she expected, to her surprise she had actually enjoyed it. I quizzed her a little further about what had been said and she told me that she thought it was very interesting to discover that Jesus had been raised from the dead. I asked her if she felt this had any relevance to her life. She responded: 'Not really, I'm not religious like the people who come here.'

I remember a boy in a school once saying, 'I know religious people believe that Jesus came back from the dead, but what's that got to do with me?'

I must say I learned something from that lady and that young boy that perhaps I should always have known. Most people are not primarily interested in whether something is true. Before they ask this question there is a far more pressing one – does it work?

Your story may not convince anyone that Christianity is true, but it may help some to see that it works. Once they have experienced this they may want to find out more about how it might work for them.

Your story is valuable because it is about what is happening rather than a set of doctrines that must be believed.

There was a time when 'evangelism' was left to the minister or preacher. The days of the great preachers live long in the memory of some and we can feel that to share faith we must be able to preach a sermon. However, the days of evangelism being done by preachers were days when the Church still had a huge influence on individuals and society. Evangelism was the job of the trained 'minister' who was to proclaim and teach the faith to the 'congregation'.

We live at a time of great opportunity – people are looking for purpose and meaning, they want to find these things but they will not come looking in church. Your story of what God is doing in your life will lead some people to want to find out more about Jesus. They are not likely to ask 'What must I do to be saved?' (Acts 16:30), but they may ask a question like: 'So how did you get into this?' or 'Have you always been religious?' They are not likely to ask the question in the way that you would ask it because they have never learned how!

So, on the assumption that you are going to take the first step and begin to talk to others about your faith, I have included some important things it is worth remembering, along with a few hints on how to tell your story.

Some important things to remember

1. 'Telling your story' does not mean just telling the person how you became a Christian. Far more important than this is what your faith means to you and why it is important to you. Talk about practical day-to-day ways that your faith helps you. It is important to do this because people will be

more interested in whether your faith is meaningful and real than how you came to believe what you believe.

It is once others have become interested in what your faith is doing that they may ask how you got it. We so often go about it backwards, we try to muster up the courage to tell people how we became a Christian before they are interested in what a Christian is. The truth is that they will not be interested in finding out how we became a Christian because many of them will assume that being a Christian just means being religious. It is only as they understand what your faith is really about that they may become interested.

2. 'Hear their story', because it is as you both share what is important and what 'beliefs' or 'lack of beliefs' that you have that the conversation will become interesting. As you listen to their views, questions, challenges in life, you will be able to talk honestly about how your faith is helping you through similar issues. As the conversation unfolds you may need to be honest and admit that you still have struggles and you are not perfect. This is perfectly OK. Remember, nobody ever became a Christian because the person sharing his or her faith with them was perfect. They can't have, because none of us is perfect!

3. Through this sharing of stories you may gradually have opportunity to tell 'His' story – this may involve talking about things that Jesus said and did, it may mean talking about how you came to know Him and what you have discovered about Him.

Some helpful hints on storytelling

- Don't make a big deal of it! Talk about your faith as naturally as you talk about other parts of your life.
- Remember you have two ears and one mouth. Listening to other people as they speak will help you get to know them and how they view life – you can then relate parts of your story that are appropriate to them.
- Try to use words that a person who does not go to church will understand.

It's so easy to use jargon – just try not to but don't be paranoid about it – if you forget yourself from time to time it's not the end of the world.

- Tell the truth. It is easy when telling your story to sensationalise what you are saying so that people will find it more interesting (and perhaps find you a little more interesting). Try not to give in to this temptation – it is the *truth* that sets people free. 'Then you will know the truth and the truth will set you free' (John 8:32).
- Don't pretend that all your problems have been solved now you are a Christian. Admit that you still face challenges/have questions/get things wrong. We can sometimes believe that God can only speak through us when we are totally pure and holy. If that were so none of us should ever open our mouths. Often it is when we are most real that people see the value of our faith, not when we pretend we don't have such problems.
- Don't criticise other churches or denominations. You may have valid criticisms but this is not the time to make them. It will not help people to find out more about Jesus and become part of His Church if they hear Christians being critical of other churches!
- Only use Bible quotes if they are appropriate. It is tempting, whenever you talk about God, to keep using Bible quotes. This is likely to confuse someone who has never opened a Bible and has no idea of what is in it.

These are just a few hints and it is likely that you will do most of the things that you shouldn't as you share your story, but don't be over concerned about not getting anything wrong. God often uses us in spite of ourselves. Perhaps the most important hint is 'try to be yourself and trust God to work through *you*'.

Summary

Every single Christian and every Christian community has a great opportunity. The message of Jesus can and will change the lives of ordinary people. Now is the time for us to ensure that the lives of our communities reflect the message and that individual Christians share this message in their daily lives.

A young boy in Somerset pointed to a crucifix on the wall of a church and asked, 'Who's the bloke on the wall?' It's time he found out.

Appendix

More to Life is a resource produced by Viz-A-Viz that helps individual Christians and churches to connect with those outside the Church and share the good news. Many Christians want to tell others about Jesus but find that the hardest part is doing it.

More to Life helps because it includes professionally produced materials that can be given away to those outside the Church. These materials will encourage those who see them to want to find out more about the Christian faith.

The Materials.

A 13-minute video/ DVD and 16-page glossy magazine that are both filled with people telling their own stories of how Jesus is changing their lives today.

In addition to the video/DVD and magazines, *More to Life* contains a project guide that outlines effective ways that the materials can be used. There is also a training manual that includes practical sessions helping Christians to gain the confidence to share their faith, and present the gospel to others.

Notes

Chapter 2

1. These figures are based on research listed below:
    In 1989 the Church of England completed a report regarding church attendance by children and young people. While this report was completed 11 years back into the last century it helps to expose a trend that has continued long after it was completed. *All God's Children? Children's Evangelism in Crisis.* is a report available in book format that was commissioned by the Church of England General Synod. It was written by an ecumenical working party. It cites a survey conducted in 1955. Figures 1 to 3 are based on this earlier survey.
2. Ibid.
3. From: 'The Truth Shall Make You Free', The Lambeth Conference (CHP, 1989), p.34.
4. Ibid. p.10.
5. Ravi Zacharias, *Can Man Live Without God?* (Word, 1995).
6. Gene Edward Veith, *Guide to Contemporary Culture* (Crossway Books, 1994), p.48.
7. Ravi Zacharias, op. cit. p.12.
8. Colin Morris, *God in a Box* (Hodder & Stoughton, 1984), p.8.
9. Ibid.
10. Ibid.
11. Pat Wynne Jones, *Children Under Pressure* (Triangle, 1987), p. 93. Quoted in the report, op. cit.
12. Professor George Gerbner, cited in *The Future of Christian Broadcasting in Europe* (McCrimmons, 1990), p. 17. Quoted in the report, op. cit.

Chapter 3

1. Howard Marshall, *The Gospel of Luke* (The Paternoster Press, 1978), p.599.
2. William Hendriksen, *New Testament Commentary 'Luke'* (Banner of Truth Trust, 1979), p.745.
3. Ibid. p.746.

Chapter 4

1. Edward Backhouse and Charles Tylor, *Early Church History* (Headley Brothers, 1899), p.1.
2. Michael Green, *Evangelism in the Early Church* (Highland Books, 1984), p.135.
3. John Stott, *The Message of Acts* (IVP, 1994), p.185.
4. F.F. Bruce, *The Spreading Flame* (The Paternoster Press, 1976), p.108.
5. Ibid. p.109.
6. Charles Hodge, *Commentary on Romans* (Banner of Truth Trust, 1989), p.89.
7. William Hendriksen, *New Testament Commentary, Romans 1–8* (Banner of Truth Trust, 1980), p.126.

Chapter 5

1. F.F. Bruce, *The Spreading Flame*, op. cit., p.188.
2. Ibid., p.238.
3. Ibid., p.257.
4. Ibid., p.251.
5. Ibid., p.306.
6. Edward Backhouse and Charles Tylor, *Early Church History* (Headley Brothers, 1899), p.221.
7. Ibid., p.21.
8. M.A. Smith, *The Church under Siege* (IVP, 1976), pp.23–24.
9. Henry Chadwick, *The Early Church* (Penguin Books Ltd, 1981), p.125.
10. Backhouse and Tylor, op. cit., p.228.
11. Williston Walker, *A History of the Christian Church* (T & T Clark, 1953).

Chapter 6

1. William Cunningham, *The Reformers and the Theology of the Reformation* (Banner of Truth Trust, 1979), p.1.
2. Ibid.
3. Leonard Cowie, *The Reformation* (Wayland, 1986).
4. Roland Bainton, *Here I Stand* (Lion Publishing, 1987), p.83.
5. Original source excerpt from preface to the complete edition of Luther's

Latin Works (1545); often known as Luther's Tower Experience.

6. William Hendriksen, *New Testament Commentary, Romans 1–8*, op. cit., p.62.
7. John R.W. Stott, *I Believe in Preaching* (Hodder & Stoughton, 1982), p.34.
8. Ibid. p.42.

Chapter 7

1. Derek Tidball, *Introduction to the Sociology of the New Testament* (Paternoster Press, 1983), p.124.

Chapter 8

1. Taken from the *Penguin Book of Historic Speeches*, edited by Brian Macarthur (Penguin Books Ltd, 1996), pp.219–222.
2. Charles Handy, *The Age of Unreason* (Arrow Books Ltd, 1990), p.3.
3. Ibid., p.6.
4. Ibid.
5. Ibid., p.22.

Chapter 10

1. Taken from the *Penguin Book of Historic Speeches*, op. cit.
2   Phyllis Thompson, *Within a Yard of Hell* (Hodder & Stoughton, 1963).
3   Nelson Mandela, *Long Walk to Freedom* (Little Brown & Co, 2000), p.89.

National Distributors

UK: (and countries not listed below)
CWR, Waverley Abbey House, Waverley Lane, Farnham, Surrey GU9 8EP.
Tel: (01252) 784700 Outside UK (44) 1252 784700

AUSTRALIA: CMC Australasia, PO Box 519, Belmont, Victoria 3216.
Tel: (03) 5241 3288

CANADA: Cook Communications Ministries, PO Box 98, 55 Woodslee Avenue, Paris, Ontario. Tel: 1800 263 2664

GHANA: Challenge Enterprises of Ghana, PO Box 5723, Accra.
Tel: (021) 222437/223249 Fax: (021) 226227

HONG KONG: Cross Communications Ltd, 1/F, 562A Nathan Road, Kowloon.
Tel: 2780 1188 Fax: 2770 6229

INDIA: Crystal Communications, 10-3-18/4/1, East Marredpalli, Secunderabad
– 500026. Andhra Pradesh, Tel/Fax: (040) 27737145

KENYA: Keswick Books and Gifts Ltd, PO Box 10242, Nairobi.
Tel: (02) 331692/226047 Fax: (02) 728557

MALAYSIA: Salvation Book Centre (M) Sdn Bhd, 23 Jalan SS 2/64,
47300 Petaling Jaya, Selangor.
Tel: (03) 78766411/78766797 Fax: (03) 78757066/78756360

NEW ZEALAND: CMC Australasia, PO Box 36015, Lower Hutt.
Tel: 0800 449 408 Fax: 0800 449 049

NIGERIA: FBFM, Helen Baugh House, 96 St Finbarr's College Road, Akoka, Lagos.
Tel: (01) 7747429/4700218/825775/827264

PHILIPPINES: OMF Literature Inc, 776 Boni Avenue, Mandaluyong City.
Tel: (02) 531 2183 Fax: (02) 531 1960

SINGAPORE: Armour Publishing Pte Ltd, Block 203A Henderson Road,
11–06 Henderson Industrial Park, Singapore 159546.
Tel: 6 276 9976 Fax: 6 276 7564

SOUTH AFRICA: Struik Christian Books, 80 MacKenzie Street,
PO Box 1144, Cape Town 8000.
Tel: (021) 462 4360 Fax: (021) 461 3612

SRI LANKA: Christombu Books, 27 Hospital Street, Colombo 1.
Tel: (01) 433142/328909

TANZANIA: CLC Christian Book Centre, PO Box 1384, Mkwepu Street, Dar es Salaam.
Tel/Fax (022) 2119439

USA: Cook Communications Ministries, PO Box 98, 55 Woodslee Avenue, Paris,
Ontario, Canada.
Tel: 1800 263 2664

ZIMBABWE: Word of Life Books, Shop 4, Memorial Building,
35 S Machel Avenue, Harare.
Tel: (04) 781305 Fax: (04) 774739

For email addresses, visit the CWR website: www.cwr.org.uk
CWR is a registered charity – number 294387

Day and Residential Courses
Counselling Training
Leadership Development
Biblical Study Courses
Regional Seminars
Ministry to Women
Daily Devotionals
Books and Videos
Conference Centre

Trusted all Over the World

CWR HAS GAINED A WORLDWIDE reputation as a centre of excellence for Bible-based training and resources. From our headquarters at Waverley Abbey House, Farnham, England, we have been serving God's people for 40 years with a vision to help apply God's Word to everyday life and relationships. The daily devotional *Every Day with Jesus* is read by over three-quarters of a million people in more than 150 countries, and our unique courses in biblical studies and pastoral care are respected all over the world. Waverley Abbey House provides a conference centre in a tranquil setting.

For free brochures on our seminars and courses, conference facilities, or a catalogue of CWR resources, please contact us at the following address.
CWR, Waverley Abbey House, Waverley Lane, Farnham, Surrey GU9 8EP, UK

Telephone: +44 (0)1252 784700
Email: mail@cwr.org.uk
Website: www.cwr.org.uk

CWR CRUSADE FOR WORLD REVIVAL
Applying God's Word to everyday life and relationships

More to Life Resource Pack

Dennis Pethers

Most people today are not interested in religion or coming to church. They are interested in 'real life' stories. The *More to Life* video and magazine are filled with people telling stories of how Jesus is changing their lives today.

Pack includes two videos, two magazines and a project guide.

£32.99 (plus p&p)
Code: MTLRP

Christ Empowered Living

Selwyn Hughes

Christ Empowered Living is Selwyn Hughes' dynamic core teaching in one easy-to-digest volume.

It will transform your life with essential principles of Christian living and help develop your full spiritual potential. Discover biblical insights that will revolutionise your approach to the way you live and help to renew your mind. This new edition improves readability and gives larger margins for notes.

£7.99 (plus p&p)
ISBN: 1-85345-201-7

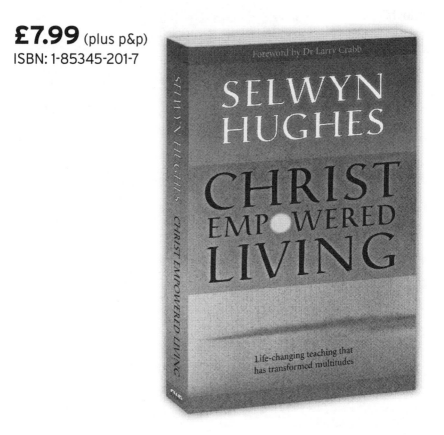

Christ Empowered Living Resource Pack

Selwyn Hughes

Selwyn Hughes' seminar, *Christ Empowered Living*, CWR's life-changing teaching, has been turned in an eight-session DVD study course for group or individual use. We are taken on a journey from the Fall to complete restoration as we learn to depend on God and accept Jesus as the power and source of life as God intended. Includes two DVDs and a workbook.

Code: CELRP

£59.99

(plus p&p)

Additional workbooks available
ISBN: 1-85345-328-5

£5.99 (plus p&p)

Walk the Walk

Pete Gilbert

This is a book on radical holiness through discipleship. Pete Gilbert says now we need 'to turn words into action, talk into walk to get what God has put on the inside of us outside' so that we do not only believe and experience it but we live it out and give it away.

£7.99 (plus p&p)
ISBN: 1-85345-321-8

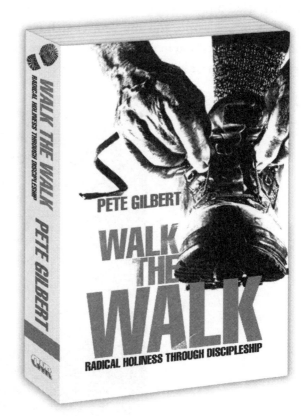

Experiencing God Together

Henry and Melvin Blackerby

*'When God's ideal is realised, the impact upon an individual,
a church, a community or a nation will be enormous.'*
Henry Blackerby

God saves individuals but places them in community with one
another. Read how through this community He can accomplish His
purposes in our world. You and your church family can experience
the fullness of life, God in your midst, and a love that can only come
from above when we experience God together.

£7.99 (plus p&p)
ISBN: 1-85345-333-1

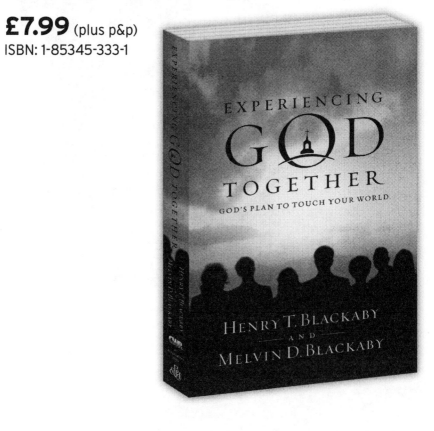